E 63   Broadhurst

THE HERRING

This medal was issued by Charles I. to commemorate the treaty (1636) between the English and the Dutch by which the latter were to pay £30,000 for permission to fish in the British Seas.

THE HERRING;

ITS EFFECT ON THE
HISTORY OF BRITAIN:

BY

ARTHUR MICHAEL SAMUEL

"Le hareng est une de ces productions dont l'emploi
décide de la destinée des Empires."—LACÉPÈDE.

"He who draws a fish out of the sea draws a piece of
silver."—FRANKLIN.

LONDON
JOHN MURRAY
ALBEMARLE STREET, W.
1918

TO MY CHILDREN; MAY
THEY NEVER FORGET
THE EAST ANGLIA OF
THEIR FATHERS.

TO THE READER

No one who studies national economics of past centuries can fail to be impressed by evidences of the close connection between the foreign policy of England and her national trade interest, though during the nineteenth century that connection was growing looser, and, in the two or three decades just before this war, had begun to disappear. Wool and herring in the period covered by the twelfth to the seventeenth centuries were what would now be called key industries. It was on them our national policy may be said to have largely turned whenever the rulers of England entered upon discussions, peaceful or warlike, with other nations. Further, our political action, whether in respect of domestic or foreign policy, was silently but ultimately based upon that national system of economics which was for the most part represented by the words wool and herring.

Norwich and Yarmouth, the two sister trade-centres of my native county, were so intimately identified with the one and the other that any investigation of the archæology of Norfolk brings the student face to face with these industries in their various aspects ; I was therefore in a position to get together much curious information on these subjects before the war brought other duties. But as the importance of the herring and its influence upon the destiny of Britain do not appear to be widely enough recognised, I have now ventured to gather my notes together and place them in book form for the use of those who may be interested in certain matters brought into prominence by the war.

It will be seen that the subject of the herring has two main aspects : its relation to the food supply, and its influence upon English, and later, British, navigation policy and the early stages of the building-up of our mercantile marine. The relation of the herring to the navigation policy of this country, in other words to our naval supremacy and commercial expansion, has a peculiar interest at this moment because we are once again confronted with a bald demand from Central European Powers expressed by the phrase " Freedom of the Seas " as employed by Germany and Austria and supported by the Papal Note. It is difficult to get at a real definition of our enemies' demand or what lurks behind it. By implication, of course, Britain is charged with violating the principle of the free use of the high seas by all nations in times of peace. What is the meaning of a charge so grotesque ? Must not the phrase therefore relate to war rather than to peace conditions ?

Britain is an island, notwithstanding aircraft and submarines.

The sea is our frontier, the cradle of our freedom; our national temperament has been created by the sense of security arising from the consciousness that we can, by our command of the sea, frustrate any attempt at invasion, as another nation protects its frontier by a line of forts. History has shown that command of the sea is command of the land; that the sea has always dominated the land; in the words of the economist, List, one of the founders of modern Germany :—

" The Sea is the High Street of the Earth. The Sea is the parade-ground of the Nations. . . . The Sea is, so to say, the rich village Common on which all the economic Peoples of the World may turn their herds out to grass. The man who has no share in the Sea is thereby excluded from a share in the good things of the world ; he is the stepchild of our dear Lord God."

Whatever may be the aerial developments of the future, the seas and the sea communications are to us exactly what land frontiers are to continental nations, and of these truths we must never for an instant lose sight. For those frontiers we fought and conquered in the seventeenth century when the principle involved was covered by the words " *Mare clausum*," of Selden, as against the " *Mare liberum*," of Grotius, and the herring fishery was a crucial point in the dispute. The question, indeed, came to a head a few years earlier, when, in 1602, the King of Denmark sought to prevent the English from fishing in the high seas, and it was one of the last public acts of Elizabeth to instruct her ambassadors to declare that the law of Nature allowed fishing in the sea anywhere, and the using of ports and coasts of princes in amity for traffic and shelter against peril of the sea, unless there was a contract to the contrary. At an earlier date the navigation of the Indian seas had been the subject of bitter dispute between the Dutch and Portuguese, owing to the grant by the Pope to the Portuguese of an exclusive right of navigation within certain boundaries. The Spanish jurists also denied the Portuguese claim to ownership of the seas, and Grotius only carried a similar line of argument further in denying that any maritime State possessed right of dominion of the waters adjacent to its territory. The student would do well to refer to a masterly essay on the whole subject contributed by Sir John Macdonell, K.C.B., to the *Nineteenth Century* for November, 1917.

Until the beginning of the seventeenth century the claims of England, even over the narrow seas, were scarcely insisted upon, and, generally speaking, the policy advocated by Selden in *Mare clausum*, his official reply to Grotius' *Mare liberum*, was kept in abeyance by James I., as the King of England owed a sum of money to his father-in-law, who happened to

be also the protesting King of Denmark. It was
Elizabeth not Grotius that first gave support
to the doctrine of the Freedom of the Seas
in the true and literal sense of the words. But
the meaning of the words as used by the jurist is
entirely different from that implied by our
enemies in 1917. German and Austria are
in fact employing the phrase " Freedom of the
Seas " in a manner diametrically opposed to the
meaning put upon it in the sixteenth and
seventeenth centuries, possibly with the intention of confusing the issue at an opportunity
convenient to themselves. Until war was
declared in 1914 the high seas were perfectly
free to the passage of all in the precise sense
of the words "*Mare liberum*," as understood
and used by Elizabeth and Grotius and by
the French in the time of Napoleon. Now,
as far as Britain is at all events concerned,
the phrase " Freedom of the Seas " is for the
most part endowed by our enemies with a
meaning contrary to the original sense. Let
there be no mistake about it. It is beyond
dispute that the sense in which the words
were understood by Grotius obtained till the
outbreak of the war, but it seems that
since then the expression is intended by our
enemies to include their right to sow mines
in the seas in time of war, and this view of
their case is supported by the reports of the
proceedings at the Second Hague Conference
in 1907. Our enemies would also force us to

surrender our overseas naval bases. Germany
seeks to increase her own sea power and
strength of naval attack and, at the same time,
to prevent Britain from enjoying the advantages
in war time of her membership of and communication with that association of scattered sister
States called the British Empire. Germany
would thus mean that the freedom of the seas
includes the domination of the seas by Germany; she would make the seas free for
Germany by dominating them herself. She
throws dust in the eyes of the world by ignor-
ing the fact that before the war she, like every
other nation, had complete freedom to use
the seas outside territorial waters for peaceful
purposes. Can she deny it ? Germany also
means by the expression, according to a recent
work by a German publicist, F. Naumann, that
she claims the right of entry in peace time into
British ports by German ships and German
cargoes on the same terms as British ships
and British cargoes. Unreasonable as such a
demand would be if made in the negotiations
for peace, it is none the less a fact that Germany
actually enjoyed those very advantages in the
ports of the United Kingdom till war was
declared in 1914, as a result of the repeal of the
Navigation Acts in 1849 ; indeed, she actually
received preferential treatment over our own
shipping. For example : German ships were
allowed to carry transatlantic passengers to
and from England and embark them or dis-

embark them off the Isle of Wight without paying full harbour dues to the port of South-ampton. German ships were allowed to carry British mails and to take them up and put them ashore off the Isle of Wight in a way which strained the provisions of British regulations. I made this statement to the President of the Board of Trade and to the Secretary of State for the Colonies at the Colonial Office on April 3, 1916, and it has never been contradicted. When considering, therefore, the disputes of the seventeenth century in which Grotius and Selden were the protagonists, the student must bear in mind that the words " *Freedom of the Seas*," as used to-day by our present enemies, have for Britain an entirely different meaning from that put upon them in the " *Mare liberum* " and " *Mare clausum* " arguments. Such being the case our business is, as Blake said in 1653, to keep foreigners from fooling us, and to remember Selden's observation that the English people are many times in treaties overmatched by them whom they overmatch in arms.

And there are other points to be considered.

The modern gun will carry twenty miles, and as the three-mile limit was presumably based on the range of a gun being under three miles, the limit of what ought to be considered territorial waters has become obsolete, or at all events inapplicable to modern conditions. Again, such questions as the use of sunk mines for coast defence, the submersion of a submarine

within territorial waters and the activities of
aircraft high above or only just over the surface
of the sea and nearer land than three miles,
put a fresh complexion upon the operation of
the principle of the three-mile limit, on the
definition of the words " territorial waters,"
and on questions depending upon that definition, such as the herring fishery.

May I express a hope that a perusal of this
book will stimulate examination of Germany's
continuous wail about the freedom of the
seas ? It is a fraudulent grievance, but none
the less it should be tested and then nailed to
the counter as spurious. We do not pay
enough heed to what may be roughly described
as British Navigation policy ; the action of the
British Government in trying to force the
Declaration of London (1909), on the country
just before the war is proof positive of this.
The Foreign Office had forgotten that Britain
is an island, and the average man cared or
knew so little about our dependence upon sea
power and communications that, but for the
stand made by certain far-seeing public-spirited
men and Chambers of Commerce, we should
ourselves have done ourselves untold mischief.
Germany sees plainly enough that loss of her
overseas trade means her ruin. She groans
about after-war facilities in our ports and
coaling stations, detecting the dangers of her
position in the markets overseas, while we
have scarcely recognised how full of advan-

tageous possibilities the situation is for us—
provided we exercise our national rights in
questions concerning mercantile shipping, and
frame our foreign policy to support our trade
policy. I am firmly convinced that the safest
basis of our economic future in relation to
our present enemies will be found to lie in a
wise attitude on our part towards their after-
war sea-carrying trade. The Central Powers
must export or perish. A very large part of
Germany's pre-war export trade was seaborne.
There is also the indispensable need of the
Central Powers for the raw productions of the
British Empire. These will be seaborne from
British imperial ports ; they provide a lever of
immense power to us.

The policy of Britain which culminated in
Cromwell's wresting their sea-carrying trade
from the Dutch began with squabbles about the
herring fishery, or in other words, about one of
our key industries. Apart from recognising the
importance of the herring in relation to food
supply, an investigation of the history of the
herring fishery and its bearing upon the destiny
of Britain will, it is hoped, help the reader to
compare what happened in the past with the
recent demand by the Central Powers for what
they call the Freedom of the Seas, whether in
time of peace or war, and will, in addition, dis-
close how vital to their economic existence they
consider the question of sea communications.

Many of my notes were made years ago,

without any idea of publication, while I was reading over a wide area for my own private instruction. I am therefore unable to remember or indicate the origin of a number of my observations or to check their accuracy. May I then ask the reader to accept this book on the following terms ?—

(*a*) That I do not profess to be perfectly accurate, although what is herein stated is, so far as lies in my power and knowledge, there or thereabouts correct.

(*b*) That I acknowledge my indebtedness to innumerable ancient and modern writers for the entire information now presented, and that nothing herein is my original work. Where the knowledge is derived from standard works of reference I have not included their titles in the bibliography. To the unknown author from whom I have taken information and incorporated it in my notes, and to the author to whom I have not given acknowledgment in the bibliography, owing to lack of records of origin, I raise a high altar and pile upon it offerings of gratitude and humble apology.

ARTHUR SAMUEL.

48, MONTAGU SQUARE,
    MARBLE ARCH, LONDON, W.
        January, 1918.

CONTENTS

PAGE

PREFACE vii

LIST OF ILLUSTRATIONS xix

CHAP.
I. INTRODUCTORY 21

SECTION I. THE HERRING AND
ITS ENEMIES 27

SECTION II. PROCESSES OF PRE-
PARING THE HERRING . . 34

SECTION III. SUPERSTITIONS
CONNECTED WITH THE HERRING 42

SECTION IV. GENERAL REMARKS 47

II. THE HERRING IN HISTORY . . 57

III. THE HERRING FISHERY . . 101

SECTION I. THE DUTCH FISHERY . 101

CHAP.   PAGE

      SECTION II. THE DUTCH AND
      ENGLISH QUESTION IN THE
      SEVENTEENTH CENTURY . 106

      SECTION III. THE ENGLISH HER-
      RING FISHERY IN THE EIGH-
      TEENTH CENTURY . . . 125

      SECTION IV. THE QUESTION OF
      PRESERVATIVES . . . 144

IV. THE HERRING INDUSTRY IN THE
      NINETEENTH AND TWENTIETH
      CENTURIES 165

      SECTION I. THE NINETEENTH
      CENTURY 165

      SECTION II. THE TWENTIETH
      CENTURY 169

APPENDICES 176

BIBLIOGRAPHY 188

LIST OF ILLUSTRATIONS

MEDAL ISSUED BY CHARLES I., 1636   *Frontispiece*

                                            FACING PAGE
* THE PLACE TO MAKE RED HERRINGS   .   34

MAKING RED HERRINGS   40

> This plate shows the master smoker, who keeps up the
> fire ; smokers to withdraw the herring from the brine
> and put them to drain in baskets ; women who string
> them on wands and hand them to men who hang them
> in the "loves" (louvres), and men who take them
> down when sufficiently smoked. The herring are then
> examined by a man who counts them before passing them
> to be packed in barrels and rejects defective fish. (From
> Du Hamel du Monceau. See Bibliography.)

MAP OF ABOUT THE YEAR A.D. 1000,
LOOKING SOUTHWARDS AND SHOWING THE
ESTUARY OF THE YARE FROM NORWICH
TO THE SANDBANK UPON WHICH YAR-
MOUTH NOW STANDS (FROM IVES' "GARIA-
NONUM")   62

* THE HULK, OR GREAT HOY, UPON HERRING
FISHING PLACE   76

* THE HERRING BUSSE SAIL'S INTO HARBOUR   93

* Those illustrations marked with * are from de Jong, Kobel
and Salieth's book (see Bibliography), 1792, drawn by S. V^dr.
Meulen, engraved by A. Van der Laan, and published by P.
Schenk.

B 2

FACING PAGE

* THE HERRING BANKET OR FEAST   .   . 104

MEDAL ISSUED IN 1630 TO ASSERT THE
  CLAIM OF ENGLAND TO THE DOMINION
  OF THE SEA   110

MEDAL RELATING TO THE ILL-FEELING
  BETWEEN THE ENGLISH AND DUTCH, 1662   110

* THE HOOPING OF HERRING BARRILS   .   116

* THE PACKING OF THE HERRINGS INTO THE
  BARRILS   126

* THE MENDING OR REPAIRING OF THE
  BROKEN HERRING NETTS   .   .   . 133

* DEEP WATER, SHORE, STATE, AND OTHER
  RED HERRINGS 154

* THE SELLING OF THE HERRING   .   . 164

* Those illustrations marked with * are from de Jong, Kobel
and Salieth's book (see Bibliography), 1792, drawn by S. V^{dr}.
Meulen, engraved by A. Van der Laan, and published by P.
Schenk.

THE HERRING

CHAPTER I

INTRODUCTORY

A YARMOUTH CHANTY.

The farmer has his rent to pay.
  Haul, you joskins, haul.
And seed to buy, I've heard him say.
  Haul, you joskins, haul.
But we who plough the North Sea deep,
Though never sowing, always reap
The harvest which to all is free,
And Gorleston Light is home for me.
  Haul, you joskins, haul.

THIS old chanty, sung by the East Coast fishermen whose chosen instrument is the accordion which they call a " mewsic," conveys an economic truth, a reminder that we do not sufficiently avail ourselves of a harvest which can be obtained merely for the gathering. The Homeric phrase " the unharvested sea " is still too true, and that at a time when the problem of the food supply of these islands is more acute than it has been for a century; though, from causes connected with the war, the harvest is less free than usual. " Joskin " is a jesting name used in East Norfolk to describe men who work on the land in summer, and go to sea " a-fishin' " in the autumn and winter. The world knows no braver men than

our fisher-folk, as their work in lifeboats and
in mine-sweeping bears witness. Many of
these excellent, industrious and fearless men
are total abstainers, and deeply religious. The
bulwark of the nation, they have never been
more valuable than they are now, and it is
the herring fishery, " the fruitful nursery of able
seamen for the navy and mercantile marine,"
which has trained them to be the safeguard
of Britain to-day.

The seas around our shores teem with fish.
Sir John Lawes once stated that an acre of
sea off the East Coast yields as much good food
for human consumption as a hundred acres of
Northamptonshire grass-land ; and the most
valuable food to be found in our seas is the
herring (*Clupea harengus*).

The market value of the herrings brought
in to the Aberdeenshire coast in a single season
was stated some years ago to exceed the annual
rental of the land of the whole county of Aberdeen, and the North Sea alone produces more fish
than all the other fishing grounds exploited by
Europeans put together. In 1908 it yielded
about 1,000,000 tons of fish, of which more than
half (57 per cent.) or 38 per cent. of the whole
value, were herrings caught in drift nets. Great
Britain catches and brings to its ports two-
thirds of all the herrings caught, and nearly
all the fish caught with the trawl ; yet,
although we are the greatest capturers of
herrings in the world, we import about 40 per

cent. of the herrings we consume; and that is so although the various fisheries of the United Kingdom provide about 85 per cent. of all the fish eaten in the country, apart from canned fish imported from North America. This astonishing fact is accounted for by the inner workings of the herring trade, and by the varying dates of the herring seasons off the coasts of the different countries.

There are in existence books, pamphlets, reports, Acts of Parliament having reference to the herring, sufficient in number to stock a good-sized library; it is not my purpose, therefore, to attempt to add anything to the exhaustive information already available, nor, indeed, is it within my power to do so. My native Norfolk love for the herring as part of my daily sustenance has led me to make rough notes of historical and other references to the subject that have come under my notice from time to time, while studying the navigation laws, our foreign policy, and the early history of our trade. Additional material came to hand recently after I had been requested to act as spokesman of the Association of Chambers of Commerce of the United Kingdom on a deputation to the President of the Board of Trade, Mr. Runciman, M.P., and the Secretary of State for the Colonies, Mr. Bonar Law, M.P., at the Colonial Office, April 3rd, 1916, on the subject of Navigation laws; and again when a similar honour was allotted to me at the Board of Trade before the President, Sir Albert Stanley, M.P., on May 16th, 1917, on the subject of the Coastwise Trade of Great Britain. On both occasions, at the wish of Sir Algernon Firth, President of the Council of the Association of Chambers of Commerce, I drew up, for the use of Ministers, on behalf of the Association, recommendations as to the future mercantile shipping policy to be observed by Great Britain and the Dominions in conjunction with their Allies, based on the study of the early history of our trade and navigation. The replies delivered by Mr. Runciman, Mr. Bonar Law, and Sir Albert Stanley, and copies of the Memoranda handed to them by me, may be found in the printed Reports of the Proceedings of the Association of Chambers of Commerce of the United Kingdom, April, 1916, No. 619, and May, 1917, No. 631.

The glitter of the herring's livery of green and silver catches the eye all through the records of British commerce and national history. Now that, owing to the German submarine menace, the shortage of food has drawn public attention to the increasing importance of fish, and especially herrings, as part of the national diet, I venture to print my notes in the hope that they may be of some interest to a generation which has, for the first time, come into personal contact with the problem of the national food supply, and more particularly to

show the part played in the history of England
by the herring in the development of our trade,
the creation of a mercantile marine, a navy,
and a Colonial Empire which, rousing the envy
of Germany, caused her to plot our destruction.
These notes may also enable the student to
grasp what Germany means when she talks
about the Freedom of the Seas.

Much of the information has been extracted
in a somewhat disjointed way, not only from
recent essays and reports on the herring, but
also from works on political economy, from
Acts of Parliament and other indications of the
national policy during the twelfth to the
nineteenth century, from commercial histories,
archæology, and standard works of reference
and from old political tracts and pamphlets.
I cannot lay claim to any original research.
The natural history of the herring has for the
most part lain outside my province. I make
no attempt whatever to construct a story or to
give these notes a dramatic interest. The notes
are merely collected and published to provide
a record of information in condensed and handy
form.

During the year January 1st, 1913, to December 31st, 1913 (if I may be pardoned a personal reference to show a comparison between
consumption and supply), I ate 161 herrings
in one form or another, but, being a Norwich
man, principally as bloaters, and I suppose
that has been my average yearly consumption

for the last thirty years or more, making a total of some 5,000 herrings. This sounds somewhat alarming, but as the average roe of a full-grown female herring contains about 35,000 eggs, human consumption is not likely to overtake the fecundity of the fish, even if half the population were to follow my example. In 1881 Professor Huxley stated at Norwich that 2,500,000,000 herrings were taken out of the North Sea and the Atlantic every year, and that over 500,000,000 herrings are contained in *one* square mile of one of the many shoals which approach not only the coasts of Britain, but also those of Scandinavia and the Baltic, and of Eastern North America, every spring and autumn. A shoal usually covers half a dozen square miles, though it may be very much larger; it is often eight or nine miles in length, three or four miles in breadth, and of unknown depth, the fish being closely packed like sheep in a flock moving along a country lane. Allowing about a cubic foot of space for each fish, we may get an idea of the size of such a shoal by imagining an area in London extending from the Albert Memorial to the Tower, and from Westminster Bridge to the Zoological Gardens, entirely covered with herrings, swimming, in compact formation, on one of those migrations which baffle understanding. The search for food is not the complete explanation. Well might Huxley say that the sum total of the herrings that inhabit our seas surpasses human imagination, and that any one shoal would go a long way towards supplying the whole of man's annual consumption.

The usual size of the East Coast herring is 10 to 11 inches, and its weight when full about 8 or 9 ounces; a herring 17 inches long is, however, on record, but 14 or 15 inches is quite an exceptional size.

SECTION I.—THE HERRING AND ITS ENEMIES.

The " herring "—the word can perhaps[1] be traced back to a Teutonic origin based on " harya " = an army—a shoal; modern German, " Heer " = an army—must not be confused with the sprat, pilchard or whitebait. Some writers wrongly regard the sprat (*Clupea spratus*) as an early stage of the herring and of the pilchard (*Clupea pilchardus*), from both of which it is distinct in kind. Again, whitebait (*Clupea alba*) is a definite species, not merely the young of the herring.[2] Shoals can be detected by the presence of a whale, of dogfish, and of predaceous aquatic birds, such as gulls, and gannets. Floating on the water over or, if moved away by the tide, near the shoal, is usually what is known as " the spot of oil " given off by the fish.

Whales, seals, porpoises, dogfish, cod, whiting and aquatic birds devour myriads of herring. Wilson in his " Tour Round Scotland

[1] Skeat is not satisfied with this derivation.
[2] For a full history of these fishes the reader should consult the pages of Jonathan Couch.

and the Isles " (1842) states that there are 200,000 Solan geese or gannets in the colony of St. Kilda alone, each goose consuming on an average five fish a day. The gannets feed at St. Kilda for about seven months each year, and in that time would, he estimates, devour 200,000,000 herring.

The dogfish, detested by fishermen, however, is probably the herring's worst enemy. He bites the herring in two before swallowing it, destroying more fish than he eats, and even breaking the fishing nets in the violence of his pursuit.

Off the east coast of Scotland dogfish from 24 to 30 inches long are caught. They have rough skins and spikes, and are known as pike dogfish. For trade purposes they might be called "sea-pike." Fishermen say that dog-fish chase the herring toward the shore, and, when wantonly destroying their prey, allow the dead fish to drop to the bottom. The Dutch, knowing that herrings, keen of sight and smell, dislike water polluted by dead fish or fish offal, forbade the gutting of herring at sea, and the disposal of the offal near certain herring grounds, as early as the seventeenth century. Yet another cause of pollution can be traced to the large spreads of nets that from time to time get adrift in storms, and are lost; if they are full of captured herrings the fish die in the nets, and their decaying bodies pollute the water. The shoals will leave the spot, and shun the district for many years. The pollution of water over a large area, owing to decaying fish in lost nets, may be one of the causes for what are called the capricious migrations of herring. It is an established fact that herrings shun waters polluted by decaying fish or offal, and for years instinctively retain their dislike of the district.

Again, if herrings that have been landed are, for any reason, allowed to lie on the seashore and become putrid, the drainage from the rotting fish will gradually reach any fishing ground close at hand in the neighbouring inlets of the sea. If the drainage from the putrid fish is appreciable in volume it will pollute the water and scare away the herring, who will not in many cases return till after the lapse of a long period. The dislike of fishermen to know of, or see, herrings used as manure is undoubtedly based upon a latent human instinct which unconsciously avoids doing anything likely to pollute the waters in which the fish normally congregate.

Yet the dogfish has his merits, and they are all too little recognised. The Americans, following the policy which is associated with the practice of utilising every portion of the pig except the squeal, have turned him to account by christening him " grayfish " and canning him for human consumption, thus at the same time lessening one of the natural causes of pollution of the seas and adding to the national food supply. The American public, according to the *Fish Trades Gazette* of March 31st, 1917, eat the canned " grayfish " as eagerly as the dogfish eat the herring, and the present demand in the United States is ten times the available supply. It may not be amiss to say that the " grayfish," when canned, provides about the same amount of nutriment as canned medium-grade salmon; the flesh is almost entirely free from uric acid, small quantities of which are present in all meats and poultry, and in most other fishes. The energy value per lb. of British-caught dogfish is 827 calories—a very high value, nearly as high as that of the best parts of salmon, and about the same as the average of beef, veal and mutton. The British dogfish should be called by an attractive name, and eaten; the energy value of its flesh being higher than that of the fresh herring, except the Shetland " mattie," but lower than that of the herring in a preserved state.

Whales, gannets, and dogfish are not the herring's only enemies, since full-grown cod also are believed to feed chiefly on herring. In most years 5,000,000 cod, ling and hake are taken by Scottish fishermen, and allowing the very small ration of two herrings a day, these fish alone would consume over 3,500,000,000 herring in a year. The Norwegian fishermen of Lofoden are said to capture 20,000,000 codfish annually, which on the same calculation would devour 14,000,000,000 herring; and the calculation is certainly too moderate, since it is no uncommon thing to find ten or twelve herring in the stomach of one codfish.

Beam trawl nets again, if used on hard bottoms, destroy a large amount of herring spawn; but against this it must be remembered that the trawl captures quantities of flat fish which devour the spawn voraciously, congregating on the spawning grounds for the purpose. Every flat fish caught by the trawl is therefore a destroyer of herrings, a worse enemy, probably, than the trawl net itself.

The herring in shoals approach our shores both in summer and winter. The summer shoals spawn near the shore at about Michaelmas, and the winter shoals about Ladyday.

Warm nights with the temperature of the water at about 55° or 56° F. are the best for catching herring, and the milder the night, the better the fish rise. When snow is on the ground the herrings swim near the shore, and the fishermen like to see snow on the hills during the winter fishing. It is probable that among the principal causes for the migration of the herring and the fluctuations of the herring fishery is the temperature of the water, which depends upon the variations of the great oceanic currents that form the Gulf Stream. Herring rise towards the surface in the dark, and till about 1905 were generally caught in drift nets. About 1905 fishermen from Milford Haven and Fleetwood began to capture considerable quantities of herring by trawling from steam trawlers in daylight from Barra Head southwards to the north-western coast of Ireland. The method was not successful at night. Trawling for herring gradually became general in the North Sea. In 1912 three per cent. of the total weight of herrings landed was captured in trawl nets. Steam and joint stock enterprise have revolutionised sea fishing during the last thirty years.

The direction of the wind seems to have some effect upon the catches of herring. Large catches are not made in calms, or during northerly winds, and the best are made when the wind is S.S.E. Unsettled water is far preferable to clear, as is a green sea to a blue, from the fishermen's standpoint, but a series of violent thunderstorms has been known to frighten the fish away from a district.

The following is a list of the herring fishings with their dates :—

ENGLAND.—East Coast *Spring* fishings at Shields and Lowestoft, but neither is of great importance, the chief fishings being in the late summer and autumn. *July* and *August :* Berwick, Seahouses, Blyth, Shields, Hartlepool, Scarborough, Grimsby, Whitby. *August* to *Christmas :* Yarmouth and Lowestoft, South and South-West Coasts. Yarmouth " longshore " herrings are caught early in September. *October* and *November :* Folkestone and Hastings. *November* to *January :* Torbay, Plymouth, Newlyn,

St. Ives, Port Isaac. *June* to *August:* Peel and Port St. Mary (Isle of Man).

SCOTLAND.—*January* and *February :* Stornoway, Campbeltown, Wick, Anstruther, Dunbar, Eyemouth and the Lochs, and some seasons at Buckie, Fraserburgh, Peterhead, and Aberdeen. There is comparatively nothing done in March and April. *May* and *June :* Stornoway, Castlebay, and Loch Fyne— the latter continuing more or less all the summer. Shetland fishing begins about the second week in June, and of late years it has continued to August. *July* and *August :* The great herring fishing along the whole of the East Coast of Scotland from Wick to Eyemouth. The chief ports are in the order given, viz., Fraserburgh, Peterhead, Wick, Aberdeen, Montrose, and Eyemouth.

IRELAND.—The summer fishing begins as early as February 1st, but is not general until about April and May. In those districts where the season begins in February it finishes at the end of March, the general fishing closing about July 31st. The autumn herring season opens during the first week of August and continues until the following January. The chief herring fishing ports are : Bantry, Castletown-Berehaven, Baltimore, Castletownsend, Kinsale, Dunmore (May and June), Arklow, Howth, Ardglass, Greenore (June and July). On the Donegal coast at Downings Bay and district the early season begins at the end of April and continues through May and June, and in some seasons there are good fishings in November and December.

The Norway herring season opens about the end of December and continues until about the middle of May.

On the coast of Norfolk very few herrings are caught in January. Towards the end of

February the East Anglian fishermen begin to catch what are known as " spring herring." This fishing lasts through March, April and May. There is little or no fat or roe in the Yarmouth and Lowestoft early spring herring, but the fat of the midsummer herring is so abundant that if it be dissected in water it covers it with oil globules.

The Yarmouth and Lowestoft herrings obtainable at Norwich are usually at their best "full," *i.e.*, four weeks before they shoot their roes in autumn and late spring ; the small spring and longshore herrings being the most delicate.

The herring's own diet is not confined to one particular kind of food ; it feeds upon small medusæ, on the lesser crustacea, on its own young, on spawn ; it is even known to feed on worms and flies, and may frequently be caught by hooks baited with artificial flies intended for other fish.

SECTION II.—PROCESSES OF PREPARING THE HERRING.

It is as bloaters that herring are usually eaten in Norfolk. The Yarmouth bloater is an ungutted, unsplit herring, one-third fresh, one-third slightly salt, and one-third lightly smoked, and, to my taste, is of the right delicacy and quality only in and near Great Yarmouth ; bloaters procured anywhere else than

The Place to m

Red-herrings.

in that town or its near neighbourhood, lacking to my mind, the peculiar excellence of the fish as eaten there. Since, however, the fish begins to deteriorate rapidly in condition and flavour within five days of being taken from the sea, it is obvious that the bloater is not the most economical, though in perfection it is the most delicious, method of preparing the herring.

The word " blöta " in Swedish means to steep, or soak. In Iceland, however, the expression " blautr fiskr " meant soft fish, or fresh fish, in distinction to " harda fiskr " = dried fish, or stock fish, a common food among the Icelanders. The name " bloater " therefore indicates that the herrings were steeped, or soaked in salt water before they were smoked.

Yarmouth [1] bloaters are prepared in various ways, of which this is perhaps the best :— 29 lbs. of common salt are thrown into 71 lbs. of water in a large vat, forming a solution in which the herring will float. They are, therefore, kept down by wooden battens weighted down with bags of salt, which gradually dissolves and keeps the solution at its proper density. When the fish have become rigid the pickle is run off and the herrings are carefully separated and suspended in a current of air (for, as at the Judgment Day, "every herring must hang by its own head ") until they are removed and smoked in " loves " (louvres) for from twelve to eighteen hours, the fuel employed

[1] NOTE.—Yarmouth means Great Yarmouth throughout this book.

being oak wood, beech wood, and turf. The best way to keep bloaters fresh, after treatment, is to hang them in a current of air, but immature fish take the salt badly and will not keep. The process must have been familiar in the seventeenth century, since in Beaumont and Fletcher there is a passage : " I have more smoke in my mouth than would blote a hundred herrings " (*Island Princess*, II. 5). Again in Ben Jonson's " Masque of Augures," 17th Speech, we read, "Why, you stinke like so many bloat herrings newly taken out of the chimney."

The next best form in which this fish should be eaten is the red herring, or unsplit smoked herring, called variously the Yarmouth red herring, high dried herring, ham herring, or " militiaman." This fish is not gutted until it reaches the kitchen. The Yarmouth red herring may be eaten, uncooked, during the months of October, November and December. The skin should be peeled off, the head removed, and the fish gutted and cut across into four pieces, dusted with pepper, and eaten with bread and butter. The hard roe fish is usually the better. The Yarmouth red herring is locally sometimes called a " militiaman "; *per contra*, the vulgar Norfolk term for a militiaman in his red tunic when the writer was a youngster, was " a red herring," much as the red herrings sold by grocers in the south of Scotland are sometimes known as " Glasgow magistrates."

On the ancient arms of Yarmouth appear what are known as "Yarmouth capons," azure, three herrings argent. At a later date the herrings were dimidiated with lions' heads, the present form.

It is not, however, to a Yarmouth man that we must go for an adequate, nay, dithyrambic appreciation of the merits of the herring. Thomas Nashe (1567), the satirist, author of "Lenten Stuffe, or the Praise of the Red Herring," was born at Lowestoft, and the following are extracts, some in the original language, from his description of Yarmouth and its most famous product, the red herring, which is simply the bloater more strongly cured, the pickle having about one-sixteenth of its weight in saltpetre added; when the herring has been cured in this mixture, it must be hung in a current of air for twenty-four to forty-eight hours before being smoked :—

"A towne it is that in rich situation exceedeth many citties, and without which . . . the swelling Battlementes of Gurguntus, a head citty of Norffolke and Suffolke would scarce retaine the name of a citty, but become as ruinous and desolate as Thetforde or Ely."

"Not any where is the word seuerer practised, the preacher reuerentlier obserued and honoured, iustice sounder ministred, and a warlike people peaceablier demeanourd betwixte this and the Grand Cathay, and the Strand of Prester Iohn."

"Doe but conuert the slenderest twinckling reflese of your eiesight to the flinty ringe that engirtes it, these towred walles, port-cullizd-gates, and gorgeous

architectures that condecorate and adorne it, and
then perponder of the red herringes priority and
preualence, who is the onely vnexhaustible mine
that hath raisd and begot all this, and minutely
to riper maturity fosters and cherisheth it."

" But let none of these scumme of the subvrbs be
too vineger tarte with mee ; for if they bee Ile take
mine oath vppon a redde herring and eate it, to
prooue that their fathers, their grandfathers, and
their great grandfathers, or any other of their kinne,
were scullions dishwash, and durty draffe and swil,
set against a redde herring.   The puissant red
herring, the golden Hesperides red herring, the
Meonian red herring, the red herring of Red Herrings
Hal, euery pregnant peculiar of whose resplendent
laude and honour to delineate and adumbrate to
the ample life were a woorke that would drinke drie
fourescore and eighteene Castalian fountaines of
eloquence, consume another Athens of fecunditie,
and abate the haughiest poeticall fury twixt this
and the burning zone and the tropike of Cancer.
My conceit is cast into a sweating sicknesse, with
ascending these few steps of his renowne ; into what
a hote broyling Saint Laurence feuer would it relapse
then, should I spend the whole bagge of my winde
in climbing vp to the lofty mountaine creast of his
trophees ?   But no more winde will I spend on it
but this : Saint Denis for Fraunce, Saint Iames for
Spaine, Saint Patrike for Ireland, Saint George for
England, and the red herring for Yarmouth."

   Again :—

" There is plain witchcraft in his skin which is a
secret that all tapsters will curse me for blabbing :
for do but rub a cann or quart pot round about the
mouth with it, let the cunningest lick-spiggot swelt
his heart out, the beer shall never foam or froth in

the cup, whereby to deceive men of their measure,
but be as settled as if it stood all night."

And again :—

" It is to bee read, or to bee heard of, howe in
the punie shipe or nonage of Cerdicke sandes, when
the best houses and walles there were of mudde, or
canvaze, or poldavies entiltments, a fisherman of
Yarmouth, having drawne so many herrings hee
wist not what to do with all, hung the residue, that
hee could not sel nor spend, in the sooty roofe of
his shad a drying ; or say thus, his shad was a cabinet
in decimo sexto, builded on foure crutches, and he
had no roome in it, but that garret *in excelsis*, to
lodge them, where if they were drie let them be
drie, for in the sea they had drunk too much, and
now hee would force them doo penance for it. The
weather was colde, and good fires hee kept, (as
fisherman, what hardnesse soever they endure at
sea, will make all smoke, but they will make amends
for it when they come to land ;) and what with his
fiering and smoking, or smokie fiering, in that his
narrow lobby, his herrings, which were as white as
whale-bone when he hung them up, now lookt as
red as a lobster. It was four or five dayes before
either hee or his wife espied it ; and when they
espied it, they fell downe on their knees and blessed
themselves, and cride, ' A miracle, a miracle ! ' and
with the proclaiming it among their neighbours they
could not be content, but to the court the fisherman
would, and present it to the King, then lying at
Burrough Castle two miles off."

Nashe, in enumerating the excellences of
herrings, says :—

" A red herring is wholesome in a frosty morning :
it is most precious fish-merchandise, because it can

be carried through all Europe. No where are they so well cured as at Yarmouth. The poorer sort make it three parts of their sustenance. It is every man's money, from the king to the peasant. The round or cob, dried and beaten to powder, is a cure for the stone. A red herring drawn on the ground will lead hounds a false scent. A broiled herring is good for the rheumatism. The fishery is a great nursery for seamen, and brings more ships to Yarmouth than assembled at Troy to fetch back Helen."

At the end of "The Praise of the Red Herring," he boasts of being the first author who had written in praise of fish or fishermen : Of the latter he says :—

" For your seeing wonders in the deep, you may be the sons and heirs of the prophet Jonas ; you are all cavaliers and gentlemen, since the king of fishes chose you for his subjects ; for your selling smoke, you may be courtiers ; for your keeping fasting days, friar-observants ; and, lastly, look in what town there is the sign of the three mariners, the huff-capped drink in that house you shall be sure of always."

The kippered herring is lightly salted, dried, split open and gutted and then heavily smoked ; it is a valuable fish food, obtainable all the year round, although to some it is indigestible. Kippers, strictly speaking, should contain no roes.

The word "kipper" is derived from the Dutch "kippen"=to hatch, and is particularly applied to fish after they have spawned. In Holland, the salmon, which is almost worthless in that condition as food if eaten fresh, was

Making

herrings.

found to be good enough when cured, and the word " kipper " soon came to be applied to the cured herring.

The fresh or " white " herring, grilled and served with or without mustard sauce, is well known all over the British Isles, as is also the same fish soused in scalded vinegar and baked in an oven with slices of onion, whole peppers, parsley and bay leaves. The strong palates of our ancestors also relished mustard sauce with the cured fish. John Russell in his " Boke of Nurture " (c. 1450) recommends it as " the metest salte for salt herring." Carlyle heads a chapter in his " French Revolution " " Grilled Herrings," and refers to them as eaten with vinegar and onion and prunes.

On the coast of North America herring roe is eaten as a kind of caviare. The herrings come up to spawn in Norfolk Sound, out of compliment, no doubt, to their relations on the Norfolk coast of England, and the natives lay under water a number of little rods of pinewood with stones tied to them, upon which the fish cast their roe. When the rods are taken out of the water, covered with the roe, they have the appearance of coral ; the roe is then scraped off, and is considered to be a great delicacy, having acquired a pleasing flavour from the pinewood. The process resembles the production of shellac in India.

Section III.—Superstitions Connected with the Herring.

In Banffshire some two centuries ago, when the herring fishing was unsuccessful, effigies of men and women were burnt on suspicion of their having caused a blight on the fishing; and as late as 1855 it was recorded in the *Banff Journal* that the herring fishery having been very backward, some of the fishermen of Buckie dressed a cooper in a flannel shirt with bars stuck all over it, and wheeled him in procession through the town in a hand barrow to bring better luck.

In Norfolk, according to *Notes and Queries*, October 7th, 1865, a queer legend existed that fleas and herrings came together. As an old Cromer fisherman said, " Times is as you may look in my shirt, and scarce see a flea, and then there won't be but few herring. But when you see my shirt alive with fleas, then there is certain to be a good tidy lot of fish." It is also a common belief that herrings desert their ordinary haunts when the boats put out on the Sabbath day.

The fishermen of the Outer Hebrides object to Sunday fishing on other than purely religious grounds. They say rightly that men work better for the week-end rest to body and mind, and that if the herring are allowed to rest on Saturday night, Sunday, and Monday morning, they settle, by being left alone, take confidence, and come up to the surface better on the Monday night when the fishing is resumed. As the herring dislike noise, and are frightened by the continual disturbance, the idea of a respite or weekly close time over the Sunday is undoubtedly well founded. The Manx, Scottish, and Cornish fishermen engaged in the Manx herring fishery are so strict in regard to Sabbath observance that they remain in port from Saturday morning to Monday afternoon. English fishermen resent the loss of two nights' fishing, and occasionally have attempted to break through the custom. By the Scottish Herring Fishery Act of 1815 herring nets set or hauled within two leagues of the coast on Sundays are forfeited.

On some parts of the East Coast the shoals are believed to be led by a shad, which is then called a " demon herring."

The most interesting superstition on record comes, however, from Dr. Johnson's " Journey to the Western Isles of Scotland." " It is held," says the Doctor, who heard the legend while staying with Macleod, " that the return of the Laird to Dunvegan, after any considerable absence, produces a plentiful capture of herrings ; and that, if any woman crosses the water to the opposite island, the herrings will desert the coast. Boethius tells the same story of some other place. This tradition is not uniform. Some hold that no woman may pass, and others that none may pass but a

Macleod." To this may be added the story told by Mr. E. V. Lucas (" Highways and Byways in Sussex," 1904, p. 173) : " It was once the custom, I read, and perhaps still is, for these men (the Brighton fishermen) when casting their nets for mackerel or herring, to stand with bare heads repeating in unison these words : ' There they goes then. God Almighty send us a blessing it is to be hoped.' "

Scottish fishermen also quote the Bible as the authority for the herring deserting localities on account of " the wickedness of the people," pointing to Hosea iv. 3 : " Therefore shall the land mourn . . .; yea, the fishes of the sea also shall be taken away."

The old tenth century historian, Peter Clausson, writing of the famous herring fishery at Bohuslän, says that the fish in his time refused in certain years to visit the coasts of Norway and Sweden, and this is the reason he gives :—

" The herring have disappeared owing to magic, bad men having sunk a copper horse in the sea and thereby driven the herring away from the coast."

The subsidiary cause was "the wickedness of the people," as in the case of the present war, according to certain theories, lay and clerical. In 1549, when the herring fishing began to fail once more, the Government passed a law providing that—

" Since there is danger that God may withdraw his blessing on account of the great sins and vices of inhabitants of the coasts (of Norway and Sweden), our tax gatherers, each one in his own district, shall see to it that the people in the fishing stations lead good and Christian lives; that there is preaching every Sunday, and people exhorted to lead a godly life, so that God may be moved by the prayers of good Christians to extend his blessing to us also in the future."

There is a belief among fishermen that a herring when caught articulates a sound similar to the word "cheese." This sound is caused by an escape of air from the air bladder, or a movement of the gills. Fishermen, indeed, frequently state that the herrings "sneeze," just as Aristotle says that gurnards "grunt." The gurnard, known off the Norfolk coast as gurnet or latchet, was known to the Greeks as "lyros" and "coccyx," apparently from the noise it was said to make.

Many fish have various forms of utterance attributed to them. On the Norfolk Broads one often hears it said that an old jack pike has barked like a dog, and the same is said of the conger eel.

Red-finned herrings, called "loaders" or "kings and queens," are sometimes caught; they are regarded as an omen of a successful fishing. One of them is then taken out of the nets very carefully, prevented from touching anything made of wood, and passed round the scudding poles as many times as the fishermen desire to get lasts of herring at the next haul.

In 1587 two herrings were caught off the

coast of Norway upon the bodies of which it was thought two Gothic letters appeared. They were taken to Copenhagen, and given to Frederick II., who regarded them as an omen of his approaching death. He consulted certain wise men who interpreted the letters to mean, " You will not fish for herrings so well in future as other nations." Various other learned people, including Professors of Rostock and several of the universities of Germany, were consulted without a more satisfactory interpretation being forthcoming. A French mathematician at Copenhagen is said to have published a large volume dealing with the prophecy, while another person published a work in which he interpreted the omen as meaning that all Europe would shortly suffer a great catastrophe.

As the outcome of a quarrel about some herrings two women were accused of being witches, were tried at the Bury St. Edmunds Assizes in March, 1664, convicted, and hanged. Sir Matthew Hale, the judge, was impressed with the worthlessness of the accusation, but the jury were influenced by the opinion of Dr. Thomas Browne, " the most famous physician of his time," who happened to be in court. This was Sir Thomas Browne, of Norwich ("Religio Medici," "Pseudodoxia Epidemica," etc.). He declared that in his opinion " the devil had co-operated with the malice of the accused." With the exception of the three Exeter witches executed in 1682 these were perhaps the last persons hanged for witchcraft in England. The blood of these two women was on the head of the author of " Religio Medici "—and only about a handful of herrings.

SECTION IV.—GENERAL REMARKS.

Vast numbers of British-caught herrings " go foreign " (to use the Yarmouth expression) salted and packed in barrels, salt fish being little, if at all, eaten in Britain. On March 13th, 1917, Captain Bathurst, M.P., answering Mr. Watts, M.P., in the House of Commons, stated that the quantity of herrings pickled in brine in Stornoway alone was 75,000 barrels, and, although its export was prohibited, there was no demand in this country for this particular kind of fish, which was very cheap and good food ; he himself had eaten some of these very pickled herrings, and desired nothing better.

Of the salt itself more will be said ; Professor Hutchinson, some years ago, had a word to say about the connection between unsound salt fish and leprosy, but in these days of ample vegetable supplies we need not think twice about recommending the use of good salt fish for habitual consumption among our fellow countrymen. Sound and well cured, it is as safe as fresh fish, but fish carelessly salted deteriorates easily and quickly becomes un-sound, and is held responsible by some authorities for leprosy in Scandinavia, on the south coast of Africa, and elsewhere. The modern British palate is entirely unused to the taste of salted (pickled) herrings ; it is doubtful whether those who have been accustomed all their lives to fresh fish would eat salt fish, at least until the herrings have been well soaked before use and the strength of the pickle thereby greatly reduced. The proper distribution of fresh fish is therefore all the more important, and, generally speaking, the advantages of cheap, wholesome fish as food have never really been brought home to our working people in our inland villages and small towns away from the coast. This is owing to the want of adequate means of distribution and cheap railway rates, and the failure to preserve the fish perfectly fresh till it reaches the consumer. There should be a system of cold storage to cope with gluts of herrings ; there is no reason why a refrigerator should not be placed in every railway station throughout the country, to be supplied daily with fresh fish so that they could be available for local distribution. This would serve two purposes, placing sound, varied and nourishing food at the disposal of the population in places removed from the sea and at a distance from large cities, and replacing butchers' meat, should it be, as is very likely, as dear and scarce after the war as it is now. It is interesting to recall in this connection that " the opening of new and distant

sources of supply of provisions to the metropolis"
was placed first in the list of advantages offered
to Parliament by the Board of the proposed
London and Birmingham Railway in 1831, and
the example might well be followed in the case
of the fish supply to-day.

The average total weight of wet fish of
various kinds landed in ports of the United
Kingdom during the five years prior to the war
(1909-13), was about one and one-fifth million
tons annually, about half of which was exported and the balance consumed at home, or
destroyed. If a calculation be made on the
usual basis for reckoning, by adjusting the
account to provide for smaller consumption by
infants, children and women, and larger for
persons of " man-value," the amount of fish
consumed by each man-unit did not exceed
an average approximate amount of $1\frac{3}{4}$ ozs. per
day. That the proportion of fish food consumed per man-unit is relatively small, when
compared with the total daily consumption
of butchers' meat, bacon, ham, fowls, rabbits,
and game, can be easily observed by any
private person. If the whole population of the
United Kingdom of all ages and both sexes
be used for calculating the average at a flat
rate, the average consumption is roughly only
$1\frac{1}{2}$ ozs. per week per head : one good-sized
herring alone weighs 8 or 9 ozs.

About 100,000 tons of fish are annually
used in the United Kingdom by the fried fish

Norway. The only country which appears to surpass our own in the consumption of meat is the United States, where it equals 179 lbs. per head per annum. American authorities are agreed that a reduction by at least a half is desirable on both economic and physiological grounds. Fish, then, should replace meat to a large extent in the dietary, especially amongst those engaged in sedentary occupations, and

	Percentage of waste.	Price per lb.	Cost per lb. of fish without waste.	Food value for 1s. Calories.
Herring (salted) . .	18	4d.	4¾d.	1,670
Sprat	—	3d.	3d.	1,300
Mackerel. . . .	50	4½d.	9d.	899
Herring (fresh) . .	34	7½d.	11¼d.	704
Catfish, rock turbot, or rock salmon (bought skinned and headed) .	22	9d.	11½d.	330
Salmon	23	2s. 6d.	3s. 3d.	292
John Dory (bought skinned and headed) . . .	14	1s. 6d.	1s. 9d.	191
Cod	49	1s. 0d.	1s. 11½d.	166
Haddock	45	10d.	1s. 6d.	165

because in normal times it is the cheapest form of animal protein.

Fish, like meat, is nearly all protein and water, with a variable amount of fat. The most nourishing are those which contain the most fat—namely, salmon and turbot. Next come herring and mackerel, while hake, cod and haddock come last, containing less than 1 per cent. of fat. The food value of 1 oz. of lean beef, 50 to 60 calories, is given by 1 oz.

of salmon or turbot, or 1½ ozs. of herring or mackerel. Dr. E. L. Sprigg's table (on p. 52) shows which fish give the best value for money at the prices named.

The herring, the sprat, and the mackerel give much the best value, the salted herring being easily first at 4d. a lb., or 2d. each for good-sized fish ; at 6d. per lb. it is second to the sprat. Two herrings, or three small ones, give 600 calories, and contain 2½ ozs. of protein ; this, when added to that in the ration of bread, gives nearly all the protein which an adult needs in the day.

Salted herrings must be soaked in water three days, the water being changed four or five times each day ; or left in a basin in the sink, with the tap running slowly, for a day or more. They must then be boiled, and are excellent served, failing potatoes, with rice or beans, and margarine or butter. If properly soaked they are also good fried, baked or grilled.

Pickled herrings are used in great quantities in Italy and France. Their goodness consists in their being fat, fleshy and white, and the best fish are large, firm and dry. The most common way to cook the pickled fish is to broil or fry ; but there are other ways of dressing them :—

Baked Herrings.—Soak six herrings in cold water for twelve hours. Dry well with a cloth. Remove the heads and tails. Mix together some black pepper with six pounded cloves, salt, and mustard. Rub the fish well all over. Place them in a baking-tin, with three tablespoonfuls of salad oil. Cook until tender, turning over now and then. Serve with mustard sauce.

Fried Herrings à la Hoveton.—Soak, clean, and dry as before. Dip in butter and a little salt. Cook in a frying-pan for ten minutes, then add a cup of stock mixed with a large tablespoonful of tomato sauce. Cook for ten minutes longer. Remove from the fire. Arrange the fish in a dish. Pour the sauce over them and serve hot.

Grilled Herrings.—Remove the head and tail. Soak in water as before. Dry the fish, and then soak in milk for two hours. Beat one egg with pepper and salt (good quantity of salt) and a dessertspoonful of chopped parsley ; add an ounce of melted butter. Mix well, dip the herrings in the mixture, and roll them in maize or oatmeal flour. Now grill, turning over once or twice. Time for cooking ten to twelve minutes.

The foul, empty, or shotten herring, the last a term familiar from Shakespeare, is also known among the Dutch as " yjdel "—empty, *i.e.*, shotten, or have lately spawned. The word " ylen " is also often used, and is derived from the Dutch word " yele (haring) "—lean (herring). But the Dutch poorer classes dislike the fish in this state, though it is wholesome food when it is kippered, and I have heard in the lower quarters of Yarmouth the expression, used by an adult to a child : " I'll give you mokus and foul fish, if you don't behave yourself." The word " mokus " is used by a section of the people of Amsterdam, and on inquiring its meaning there I was told it was a corruption of the Levantine word " markoot," meaning " blows."

The word has probably come over to Yarmouth with the Dutch fishermen. Herring full of roe or milt are called by Scottish and Irish fisher- men " matties," a corruption probably of the Dutch word "matjes" or "maatjes." These Dutch phrases, now part of the language of the fisherman, prove more conclusively than any document the influence of Holland on the herring fisheries of the world.

One or two other local words may also be noted.

In 1782 the word " cadger " appeared in certain pamphlets to denote a hawker who carried fish into inland parts of the country, selling the fish for money or exchanging it for country produce, such as eggs, butter, poultry, and so on, which were in turn brought back to the towns, and sold. The exchange by hawkers or higglers of summer mackerel for eggs in mid- Norfolk is not uncommon even to this day.

The word " cadger " = hawker (carrier of a pack) has passed into common usage in an unworthy sense, as has the now nearly obsolete word " coshganger," or " cosher " (and to go " coshing ") which in East Anglia is used to denote a person who " sponges " upon another by " cadging " a meal. The word " coshganger " is of Irish origin, and was brought over by the Irish cattle drovers who attended Norwich cattle market ; it meant a country dweller who declined to perform regular work.

In the *Spectator* (No. 179), of Tuesday,

September 25th, 1711, Addison calls a merry-andrew " a pickled herring."

The fourteenth century word for curing herrings was in Dutch " kaken " = to pack in barrels, " kaecken " or " kaeckjes," whence our word "kegs." The arms of the Dutch settlement of Beuckelzen are two " kaeckmaskens," or knives used in curing herring. Our word "sloop" has the same origin as the Dutch "slabbaert," a small vessel used in the herring fishery.

CHAPTER II

THE HERRING IN HISTORY

As it has been said that the foundations of Amsterdam were laid on herring bones, so in one sense, the Civil War owed its origin to the Yarmouth fisheries, for it was to protect them and the coast trade generally that the expedient of levying " ship money " was hit upon. Nor was the danger an idle one. The Dunkirkers had been scouring the coast for some years, and on one occasion had actually landed at Tunstead, while the North Sea fishing fleet did not dare to sail without an armed convoy.

Out of the English herring fishery, again, grew the mercantile marine and ultimately, through Cromwell's Navigation laws, the British Navy. It is therefore no uninteresting task to trace the herring through history, and to note the events, social and political, connected with it, with an eye kept wryly on the seventeenth century disputes about the Dominion of the Sea. An understanding of those disputes will help us to grasp in some respects the meaning of the expression " Freedom of the Seas," as used by the Germans during the present war.

About the year 240 Solinus described the

inhabitants of the Hebrides as living on fish and
milk, and ignorant of the cultivation of grain :—

"Hebrides quinque numero, quarum incolae
nesciunt fruges, piscibus tantum et lacte vivunt."
                    SOLIN., "Polyh." c. 25, ed. Paris, 1503.

The Dutch came to Scotland in the year
836 to buy salted fish of the Scottish fishermen,
whether herring or not is uncertain, although
several writers on the herring fishery assume
this statement to prove the earliest date for
herring fishing in British waters. Swinden,
however, in his "History and Antiquities of
Great Yarmouth" thinks that the herring
fishing started at Yarmouth soon after the
landing of Cedric the Saxon in 495. He states
that the Church of Saint Bennet's was built by
Felix, the Bishop of the East Angles, in 647,
on the Greenhill, "and a Godly man placed
in it to pray for the health and success of the
fishermen," and that men came to fish at Great
Yarmouth in the herring season. A second
church dedicated to Saint Nicholas, the patron
saint of fishermen, was afterwards built in the
same place. In 709 mention is made of the
herring fishery in the Chronicle of the Monas-
tery of Evesham.

It is stated in the Saga of St. Olaf, dated
about the year 980, that Seigurd Sur enabled
his bondmen to buy their freedom by lending
them what was necessary for the fishing of
herring. About the same time, also, a herring

boat going south is mentioned in the Saga
of Olaf Tryggvessön. From 960 to 975 the
Norwegians fished the herring with large nets
in the district near Christiania, and a few
years later the abundance of fish was so great
that all the coast districts of Norway were
swarming with them, so much so that we find
Snorro, the Herodotus of the North, in 978,
referring frequently to the herring fishery on the
coast of Norway and noting the abundance of
herring and corn as characteristic of a benefi-
cent reign.

Beccles (which is not very far from Great
Yarmouth), at the time of King Edward the
Confessor paid as rent or income to the abbey
of Saint Edmond 30,000 herring, a number
increased to 60,000 in the reign of his successor.
A part of Beccles Fen near the river is called
" Solfon," which shows that it formed a salt pan
for the production of salt for curing herrings.
The salt was obtained by the evaporation of
sea water. Beccles was originally a fishing
town; but after the reign of Henry VIII.
herrings ceased to be caught near the town, as
the sea was banked out by sea walls near Great
Yarmouth.

The abbey of Saint Edmondsbury in the year
1286 expended £25 on herring for the monks
during Lent. As a fat ox was purchased for 4s.,
and as the yearly expenditure of the abbey
kitchen on all food, including fish, was £529, the
importance of the herring may be easily seen.

The earliest notice of the herring fishery in France is in the Charter of the Abbey of Saint Catherine, near Rouen, about 1030, where it appears that certain salt works near Dieppe were to pay to the abbey five milliards of herring.

There is a reference during the reign of King Macbeth of Scotland, 1037—54, to a Scottish fishery which was the basis of a small amount of export commerce, but the fish are not defined :—

> "All hys tyme wes gret plentè
> Abowndand, báth on land and se."
> *Wyntoun's Cronykil of Scotland.*

In Ives' "Garianonum" there is the following note : "Norwiz ancientment fust un lieu de Grand Fishinge. Vide Cart. Alfr. Est-Anglorum. Epi Sancto Edmundo Mansuram suam in Norwico que annuatim reddit unum lastum de Halecibus. Monast. Ang. Vol. I., fo. 294." Ives says that about the time of Edward the Confessor, 1042—66, the sea retreated from the sand at the mouth of the "Aestuary" on which Great Yarmouth now stands; "and then there were two channelles for Shippes and Fishermen to pass and enter into that arme of the sea for utterance of theire fishe and marchandizes, whiche were conveyed to divers partes and places, as well in the countye of Norfolke as in the countye of Suffolke, by reason that all the wholle level of the marshes and fennes, which nowe are betwixte the towne of Yermouthe and the citie of Norwiche, were then all an arme of the sea, enteringe within the lande by the mouth of Hierus (Yare), and this was aboute the yere of our Saviour MXL and longe before."

Yarmouth is mentioned in Domesday Book, 1086, as containing 70 burgesses, " Garleston " (Gorleston) as having three salt pans, the importance of which we shall see later ; twenty-four fishermen in Yarmouth belonged properly to Gorleston. The port of Dunwich paid, and had long paid, 60,000 herrings to the King, and that of Sandwich 40,000 herrings annually to the monks.

In 1088 Robert, Duke of Normandy, by a charter to the abbey of La Sainte Trinité at Fécamp allowed a fair to be held for one day while the herring fishing was in progress.

In 1108 Henry I. made Yarmouth a burgh, the annual payment for which was ten milliards of herring.

Herrings were among the articles charged with tolls or duties at Newcastle-on-Tyne in the reign of Henry I. Herrings, like oysters, were then very plentiful, and so highly valued that silver was brought to England from Beame (Bohemia) by way of the Rhine, in exchange for these commodities, and for wool, butter, cheese and cattle.

By the charter of King David I. to the abbey

of Holyrood, 1138, the right to fish herring at Renfrew was granted.

In 1152 William of Malmesbury calls Norwich, which was still regarded as a fishing town, though it had in fact ceased to be so, a " populous village remarkable for its merchandise." The town was rebuilt in this year, made a corporation, and given by King Stephen as an appanage to his son William.

Norwich became a free city by charter, May 5th, 1194. The charter is now in the muniment room of the Norwich Castle Museum; it bears the seal of Richard I. A new charter was given in 1404. The author of this book served (1912—13) as chief magistrate of the City of Norwich under this charter.

In 1153 among the laws of King David of Scotland dealing with commerce was one providing that all goods brought by sea should be landed prior to sale, except salt and herrings, which might be sold on board the vessels. During the same reign the Firth of Forth was frequently covered with boats manned by English, Scottish and Belgic fishermen who caught herring in the neighbourhood of the Island of May. This seems to be one of the earliest records of the herring fishery on the North British coast, but as Scottish subjects on the south side of the Firth of Forth were then called English it is open to doubt whether those whom we nowadays call English went so far from their own ports on

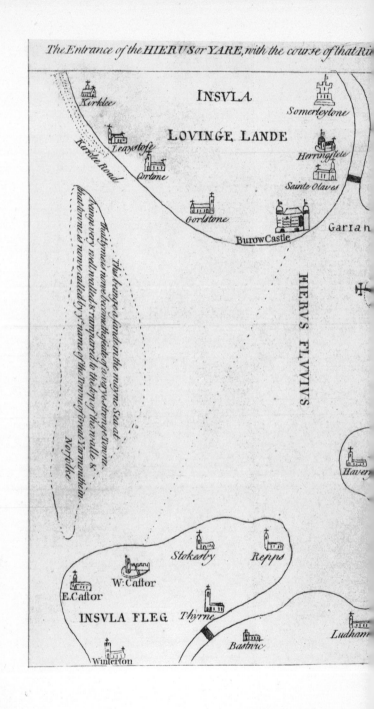

INSVLA

LOVINGE LANDE

Kirklee

Somerleytone

Karvile Road

Leaystofe

Herringflete

Ortone

Sainte Olaves

Gorlstone

Garian[...]

BurowCastle

This Longe's lande, in the mayne Sea at
Yarmouthe is nowe the syde of a very stronge Towne
beinge very well walled & rampayred: In the dyn of the walle is
that borne, is nowe called by y.º name of the Towne of Great Yarmouth in
Norfolke.

HIERVS FLVVIVS

Haven[...]

Stokesby

Repps

W: Castor

E. Castor

Thyrne

INSVLA FLEG

Bastvic

Ludham[...]

Winterton

Norwich and the Estuary of the Yare about A.D. 1000, pr[...]

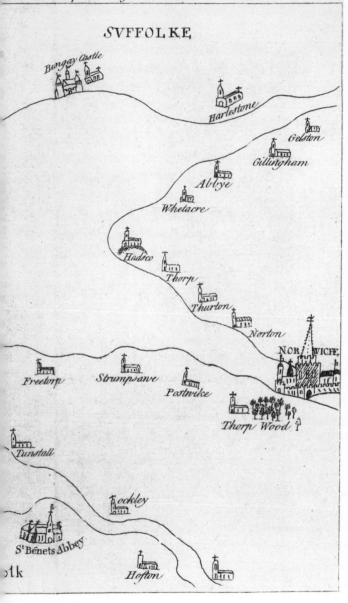

SVFFOLKE

Bungay Castle

Harlestone

Gelston

Gillingham

Abbye

Whetacre

Hadsco

Thorp

Thurton

Norton

NOR WICHE

Freetorp

Strumpsave

Postwike

Thorp Wood

Tunstall

ockley

St Bènets Abbey

olk

Hofton

stence of the town and haven of Gt. Yarmouth; looking south.
                    (Ives', *Garianonum*.)

fishing voyages to what was at that time a
hostile country.

In the reign of Henry II. herring formed part
of the revenue of the bishopric of Chichester.

In 1155 Louis VI. of France prohibited his
subjects from buying anything in the towns
of Estampes but mackerel and salted herring.

If Beuckels (see p. 101) had any merit as an
inventor it must have been in the introduction
of gutting the herring, since the "Kronikel van
Holland" tells us that in 1163 herrings were first
fished for in the Meuse, and the first fishery
established at Brielle. The fishermen of Zierik-
zee were the first to fish and pack herrings in
barrels; those of Biervliet, where Beuckels was
born, the first to make use of a better method
of preserving the fish by cleaning the insides;
while the fishermen of Zeeland, Holland and
West Friesland fitted out small vessels called
sabards or slabbaerts and joined in the fishing.

In 1187 Philip II. granted a charter to
Liège which records the town's privilege of
buying and selling fresh and salted herring.

King John in 1199 created Dunwich a free
burgh, for the annual payment of 120 pounds,
one mark of silver and 2,400 herring, a great
decrease on the payment in kind recorded in
Domesday Book.

The earliest notice of the herring fishing of
Ireland is about the year 1202, when we read
that King John confirmed a donation of herring
to the abbey of Connal.

Six years later (March 18th, 1208), the same king granted a charter to Yarmouth in which he gave permission to foreign merchants to come thither to buy herring.

In 1215 Thibaut VI., Comte de Blois, gave by charter 500 herring annually to the hospital of Beaugency.

When Princess Margaret was married to the Duke of Brabant in the reign of Henry III. the ships taking them to Brabant were furnished with 10,652 herring, 292 cod and two barrels of sturgeon.

Herrings caught about this time off the south-west coast of England were salted by an improved method by a Yarmouth man, Peter Chivalier, who appears to have held the king's licence for a monopoly of his method, which was so highly valued that Peter de Ferars of Cornwall gave the king twenty marks in the years 1221 and 1222, and, subsequently, more than once, paid the same sum for a licence to salt fish according to Chivalier's method.

In 1224 herring were so abundant on the coast of Pomerania that as many as could be carried on the back of a horse were obtainable for what would correspond to three-farthings of our money to-day.

The Hanseatic League owes much of its trade to the herring, for what really led the Germans away from their inland towns to the shores of the Baltic—and the Prussians were fishing off their own coasts in 1259—was the desire to benefit by the wealth which could be obtained for the mere fishing of its waters. In the eleventh, twelfth and thirteenth centuries, when all Europe that was not Roman Catholic belonged to the Greek Church, holy days were strictly observed, and the sale of fish was an important industry. Ice, as a preservative, was then not known, and salt was the means by which fish was kept fit for human food. From the twelfth to the fifteenth centuries the Hansards, who discovered the importance of salt for preserving fish long before the Dutch, came to the coast of Scania, the island of Rügen, and the coast of Pomerania, for the sake of the neighbouring salt springs, and as early as the twelfth century Kolberg was famous as a market for salt herring. We read in a Polish poem recording a victory there in 1105: " They brought us herring and stinking fish, and now our sons are bringing them to us fresh and quivering."

The Hansards sent herring to Germany, to Flanders and the Low Countries, to the cities of the Baltic, to Augsburg, Nuremburg, Bruges, Cracow, Breslau, and Novgorod. They exchanged English wool, hides, corn, beer, and cheese, brought to Northern Europe from their factories at Norwich and Lynn, for herring; for herring they exchanged tallow and the timber for shipbuilding brought from Novgorod; we even find the servants of the Hansa League who administered the Han-

merchant ships sailing the seas. Out of the
Dutch mercantile marine sprang Cromwell's
Navigation laws of 1651 ; out of Cromwell's
Navigation laws grew the British mercantile
marine, the nursery of the Navy ; out of the
repeal of the British Navigation laws in 1849
sprang the German mercantile marine, from
which grew the German navy, and, eventually,
the German submarine, with the result that we
are now short of bread and meat and so must
turn again to fish. And this brings us back to
the herring, the point from which we started.

The placing of herrings in barrels changed
the destinies of Holland, and with them those of
the whole world, in the sixteenth and seventeenth centuries. Well might Lacépède say :
" Le hareng est une de ces productions dont
l'emploi décide de la destinée des empires ; "
well might that wise old monarch, King
James I. of England and VI. of Scotland, who
saw what the herring had done for the " Easterlings," as the Hansards were called in England,[1] beg his friends to eat fish, and exclaim
when the Puritans gave fishing as one of the
inducements for their emigration to New
England, " Od's fish, my soul, 'tis an honest
trade. 'Twas the Apostles' own calling." This
story may have been in Marvell's mind when
he wrote in his satire on Holland (c. 1653) :—

[1] The London warehouse of these Easterlings (whence, some say,
our word "sterling"), called the Steelyard, still existed in the life-
time of James I. on the exact spot where Cannon Street Station now
stands.

" How could the Dutch but be converted, when
The Apostles were so many fishermen ? "

The Hansa League had long been a power in
London, the corporation having ceded to the
Hansards the defence of Bishopsgate. And all
this wealth and importance were based upon
the herring, two barrels of which, or a cask of
the finest sturgeon, or one hundredweight of
Polish wax, were presented by the Hansards
annually to the Lord Mayor of London, while
fifteen gold nobles, wrapped in a pair of
gloves, were given to the alderman who was
chosen to judge their disputes within the city
boundaries. The League indeed had the power
of the purse, and the art of " peaceful pene-
tration " was not discovered by the nineteenth
century German.

The best money in the Middle Ages was that
of Lübeck, and English traders stipulated that
they should be paid in pounds of the Easterlings, the pound being a Flemish reckoning
containing twenty shillings, and each shilling
twelve groats. The pound was an actual
pound weight of silver, although in the fourteenth century Lübeck was permitted to coin
gold pieces called guilders, resembling the
Florentine ducat (" florin ") the gold being
bought by the Easterlings at Bruges. The
" pound sterling " of to-day is therefore by
origin the Flemish pound of silver of the
fineness and quality used by the Easterlings
of Lübeck, the most powerful city of the

" And we will that they of the City of Yarmouth void dene and strand of old ships and timber where they should arrive and dry their nets except such ships as are being built, or masts which are being dried."

One Norfolk manor at least had the right to exact herring dues from its tenants, as we learn from an interesting MS. sold at Sotheby's on July 2nd, 1917, dating from about 1590, and entitled :

" The View of the particulars of the mannor of Shipdam as well of the rents services with other the hereditaments thereunto belonging as of the rightes apperteyneing to the same, not yet in the possession of the Lorde of the saide mannor as followith."

Shipdam is near East Dereham, Norfolk.

Among the details given we read :—

" When the Lorde lieth ther, they must not onlie doe those seruices but also make all his cariages of wyne woode *herring*, corne, haie, compace, wasshing and clipping of shepe and all service els to the number of twoe thousande seaven hundreth and fortie daies : " " the Lord hath free Bull and free Bore : " " There are nowe belonging to the saide mannor manye Bondmen."

The right is clearly far more ancient than the MS.

In 1285, Robert Durham, Mayor of Berwick-on-Tweed, ordered herrings and other fish to be sold " on the bray " alongside the vessel bringing them to port, and forbade the fishermen to carry them ashore after sundown ; any burgess who witnessed a purchase of herring might claim sufficient for his own use and consumption at the original cost.

In Blount's " History of Strange Tenure of Lands" is a quotation of a clause from the Charter of the town of Great Yarmouth (1286) requiring the corporation to send 100 herrings baked in twenty-four pasties to the Sheriffs of Norwich who were to deliver them to the Lord of the Manor of Carlton. The Sheriffs of Norwich held thirty acres of land by the service of carrying to the King of England, wherever he might be, twenty-four pasties of the fish as soon as they were in season, the herring then, and long after, being regarded as a Royal dish. An illustration of this occurs in a chronicle history of Norwich under the date 1629 :—

" The mayor and sheriffs received a letter from his majesty's secretaries of state, complaining of the quality of the herring pies, which, according to established usage, are annually sent to the king by the corporation, as the ancient fee farm of the city, and continued to this day. This was a fishing town ; the lord of the manor of East Carlton is bound to receive the pies, and carry them to the king, wherever he may then be ; this manor being anciently held of the Crown under that service. The corporation of Norwich to make and provide the pies, twenty-four in number, containing a hundred herrings, by the great hundred, in good standing pastry, and well seasoned ; and they are to be made of the first herrings which come to the city. The complaint set forth, that they were not the first herrings that were taken, according to the tenure—the pies were not well baked—the herrings were deficient in number—

an earlier date, bricks and wool.   The last is the largest unit of a peculiar system of measures, which runs :—

4 herrings equal 1 warp
33 warps   ,,   1 hundred (132 fish)
10 hundreds   ,,   1 thousand (1,320 fish)
10 thousands ,,   1 last (13,200 fish).

The word "cran," the more usual modern measure for herrings, is derived from the Gaelic word "craun" = a barrel of 36 gallons, or $3\frac{1}{2}$ cwt. of herrings.[1]   In Scotland, and at certain places in England and Wales at which the Cran Measures Act of 1908 is in force, fresh herrings are sold by the cran, containing $37\frac{1}{2}$ Imperial gallons.   In the Isle of Man and in Ireland, fish is sold by the maze, which contains five long hundreds (one long hundred equals 126).   On the east coast of England, in places where the Cran Measures Act is not in force, herrings are still sold by the last.

The following is an extract concerning the Charter of Croyland, in 1305 :—

" In the time of Yarmouth Fair, in the 34th year of the reign of King Edward, son of King Henry, William de Ketene, monk of St. Faith, and Reginald de Burgh of St. Peter, brought to the bailiffs of Yarmouth a writ of the lord the King in these words :—

Edward by the grace of God, King of England, Lord of Ireland, to his bailiffs of Yarmouth, greeting, etc.

---

[1] A standard barrel contains (1917) $26\frac{3}{4}$ Imperial gallons, and will take between 600 and 1,000 herring according to the class and size of the fish.   About 350 pickled herrings weigh 1 cwt. ; if the herrings are fresh, about 280.

An Hulk or great Ho.

Herring Fishing place.

Witness myself at Newburgh in Tyndale the 30th August in the 34th year of our reign.

By authority of which writ, the aforesaid Reginald had eight lasts and one thousand herrings delivered free of customs—viz, five lasts, and one thousand herrings for the year 34, and three lasts for the year 33—which said eight lasts and 1000 herrings, the aforesaid Reginald swore upon the Holy Bible were the property of the Abbot and Convent of Croyland, and for them were bought and provided, besides twelve pence halfpenny, which the said Reginald pledged for the aforesaid three lasts of herrings for the custom of the year 33, are delivered to the aforesaid Reginald at the request and in reverence of the said William de Ketene, monk."

A Yarmouth record of the year 1306 refers to the herring fishery. Somewhat later, in the reign of Edward III., a law was passed forbidding any fisherman to give up his trade on account of the regulations being disagreeable to him, and in return fishermen and mariners were exempt from serving in any other capacity than that to which they had been bred up.

In 1338 the same king obtained from Yarmouth 40 lasts, *i.e.*, 480,000 herrings for food for his army in Flanders.

We may judge of the importance of the export trade in herrings in the early fourteenth century from the fact that no fewer than sixty foreign vessels, of which ten were from Lombardy, procured herrings at Yarmouth harbour during the five days from September 28th to October 3rd, 1344.

Complaints having been made that the people
of Blakeney in Norfolk sold their fish too dear,
it was ordained that all fishing vessels of the
town and the adjacent coast as far as Cromer
should bring the fish to Blakeney; nor were the
fish to be carried out of the vessel till the owner
had sold them, and then only in clear daylight.
No fish might be sold by secret agreement, and
no fishermen might store the fish for sale at
higher prices later on, nor might any but a
fisherman buy hooks, nets and fishing tackle
in the county of Norfolk.

In 1357 was enacted the Statute of Herrings
already referred to. The preamble states that
the people of Yarmouth made a practice of meeting the fishing boats and buying the herrings at
sea, and that the keepers of the lodging-houses
assumed the prerogative of selling the herring
belonging to the fishermen who lodged in their
houses, paying what they thought proper for
them, thereby defrauding the fishermen and
cheating the public in resale. It was therefore enacted that no fish should be sold until
the boat bringing them was moored to land;
that the fishermen should have full liberty to
sell their fish at Yarmouth between the rising
and setting of the sun; that the price of herrings to be cured as red herrings was not to be
above forty shillings per last of 10,000; that
the pykers—vessels which carried fish between
London and other ports—were not to be
allowed to buy herrings in Yarmouth harbour

between September 29th and November 11th,
or to enter the harbour at the time of the fair,
of which the barons of the Cinque Ports were
the governors. The lodging-house keepers
were allowed to make a charge of 3s. 4d. upon
every last of herrings sold to any other lodging-
house keeper, in return for which they were to
insure full payment to the fishermen. The
people of Yarmouth were prohibited from
selling herrings for more than 6s. 8d. per last
above the price paid for them at the fair, and
the people of London were not to increase the
price by more than 13s. 4d. Shotten herring
were to be sold at half the price of full ones when
fresh, and when made red at 6s. 8d. per last
below the rate for full red herring. The pykers
were allowed to buy herring from the fishermen of " Kyrlky " (near Lowestoft), but the
fishermen could only discharge as many herring
there as would be sufficient for loading the
vessels. The rest of the fish had to be carried
to Yarmouth, no other sale being permitted
within seven leagues of the town except of
herrings of a man's own demesne fishing. The
statute also applied to any town in England
where herring were caught.

There is no doubt that the statute was passed
because the Commons complained to the King
that the people of Great Yarmouth " meddled "
with the sale of herrings, giving the fishermen
as low a price as they thought fit for the fish
by means of some tariff agreed upon among

the buyers, and charging the public as high a price as they chose by some similar arrangement.[1]   The principle of the statute was not new, since six years earlier, in 1351, a law had been passed imposing pains and penalties upon " forestallers " or " regrators " or " ingrossers " as these early dealers in " corners " were called. The statute was therefore, merely a case of applying a recognised principle to a particular industry and with special reference to a particular locality.   A " corner " in herrings existed in Yarmouth, and the statute of 1357 was passed to break it.

The statute cannot, however, have been carried out to the letter.   It is on record that in October, 1382, lodging-house keepers in Yarmouth and elsewhere were ordered to desist from their practice of manipulating the prices of herring or any other fish.

Certain modern cynics have recently observed that while trusts, rings and profiteering practised by sellers of commodities have always earned the hatred of the public, labour[2] rings and trusts, and profiteering by labour—the policy, that is, of compelling the public to pay higher prices for labour in the production of necessities—have never been regarded from the same point of view by the very people who

[1] In the same way, the great joint-stock banks of to-day, by means of a ring, or agreement, fix by advertisement the rate of interest as high or low as they think proper when taking money on deposit from the public in London, while charging for loans rates of interest fixed roughly among themselves.

[2] See *Saturday Review*, November 10th, 1917, p. 364.

complain of " profiteering " in relation to other commodities. The small shopkeeper and persons paid a fixed salary, such as clerks, however, now complain that the " war bonus " of miners and others providing necessities of life is profiteering just as much as the manipulations of food prices and the like.

We note that in 1379 Newcastle coal was favoured by the Government and taxed at a very low rate, while herrings, and the herring fishery were taxed at the highest rate; also, that in the same year Thomas Cobald bequeathed to the High Altar of St. Nicholas at Great Yarmouth, among other things, a wey of salt, while three years later, in 1382, William Rook-haghe bequeathed to the same church no less than three weys of salt gross. A wey of salt [1] consisted of 40 water bushels or 200 pecks, 5 pecks being the amount of salt required to cure one barrel containing 800 herrings.

In the same year, 1382, Philippe de Mazières states that there were many thousands of vessels, each having at least six persons on board, engaged in the fishing for herring in the seas between Denmark and Norway, that there were, in addition, 500 vessels for packing and gutting the herring, and that there were more than 300,000 persons engaged in the herring fishery.

In the " Annals of Dieppe " there is a record

---

[1] In the seventeenth century a wey of salt was worth about 40s.

T.H.   F

About the year 1397 the Fishmongers' Company of London had their privileges defined by charter, and, in the grant, the rights of the vintners to export clothing and herrings to Gascony were carefully saved.

Evidence of our dominion of the sea appears in the year 1402, when the magistrates of Bruges complained to King Henry of severe injuries to their trade, particularly to two fishermen of Ostend and Brielle in Holland, who were taken prisoners by the English while fishing in the North Sea and carried to Hull, though they had lowered their sails as a token of submission the moment the English had called to them.

The English, however, were not usually the aggressors. The correspondence between the British Government and the Hansa League in 1405 contains various complaints of injuries suffered by English subjects; among those enumerated are the grievances of a citizen of London, who had been plundered of 5 lasts of herring in the North Sound, and of four merchants of Yarmouth and Norwich, who in 1394 were robbed of woollen cloth to the value of £666 13s. 4d., which they had put on board a Prussian vessel. Injury had also been done to vessels belonging to the Norfolk towns of Cley, Wiverton and Lynn.

In 1409 the Hansards on their side were complaining that the officers of Southampton had overcharged them two shillings on every last of herrings; nor was the rivalry confined to the countries already mentioned, since in 1418 a treaty made between Louis XI. and Charles, Duke of Burgundy, provides that the French shall not molest the herring fishers of Holland, Zeeland, Brabant, Flanders and Boulogne.

In the year 1410 a Royal grant of toll was made for paving the streets of Cambridge,[1] part of the funds being supplied by a toll on the fisheries, a large boat of herrings paying fourpence, herrings a halfpenny per barrel, and porpoises one farthing each for this purpose. Porpoises were regarded as a dainty. A porpoise (entered as a "purpos"), costing xx shillings, was presented by the Citizens of Norwich to the Duke of Suffolk in 1536. A porpoise, a peacock "in hys pryde," dobyl-bere and ypocras were served at the banquets given at Norwich on Guild-days at that period by the Guild of Saint George, which was founded in 1324. In 1415, Henry V., at the request of Eric, King of Norway, prohibited the inhabitants of certain towns, among them Gernemouth (Yarmouth), Linn (Lynn), Gippeswick (Ipswich), Cranmer (near Lynn), and Dersingham, from fishing on the coasts of Norway, owing to the English having abused the permission given them in 1294.

The Scots from an early date retained the

---

[1] Here the Proctors in early days destroyed bad herrings. At the end of the eighteenth century the famous feasts of dons at Stourbridge Fair began with a large dish of herrings.

were fish markets. The measures by which the fish was sold were also fixed, and the barrels were ordered to be branded with a hot iron, the cooper's mark being set upon each ; if any barrels were unmarked the contents were forfeit, half to the king and half to the town.

In 1573 herrings were no longer allowed to be sold at sea, but had to be brought to shore, and sold in " burrowes " only. Those who happened to " slay herrings " had to bring them to free ports to be sold to the king's lieges, the measure of every barrel of herrings to be " nine gallons of the striveling measure."

Abut this time (1575) red herrings were a very common and therefore little appreciated article of food in Scotland, and the poet Montgomerie complains, in the alliterative metre that England had long outgrown :—

> " This is no life that I leid up a land
> On raw reid herring reisted in the reik."

These notes on the Scottish fisheries while the northern kingdom was still independent may be concluded by observing that in 1579 King James VI., whose comments on fishing have already been quoted, renewed the prohibition of the sale of fish " except they were landed in Scotland," so that the Scots themselves had an opportunity of buying before the herrings were sold for export. The " slayers of herrings " had to bring them to the nearest " burrowes," or the towns near to the dwellings of the " slayers," and after local needs had been satisfied the surplus might be salted and sold to strangers and for export. In 1584 a more stringent Act of the same character was passed compelling all Scottish fishermen to bring their catch to certain defined ports. Three years later it was enacted that ships fishing for herring in the North Highlands were, in return for victuals, to bring back one third part of their catch to be sold in the north isles and lochs. A law of 1600 went still further, and prohibited the export of herrings before October 11th altogether, in order that the fish might be available in the public markets of Scotland. But trade jealousy must have been very strong at the time, since much blood was shed when King James VI. endeavoured to increase the fishing stations by taking over the Lewis Islands and establishing a fishing colony among them. Another attempt was made in 1605, but the enterprise was soon afterwards given up.

Returning to the English fisheries, we find the Duke of Bedford sending 500 cart-loads of herring, convoyed by Sir John Fastolf, as food for the army under the Duke of Suffolk, which was besieging Orleans and the neighbouring towns in 1429. The French, who attempted to capture this convoy at Rouvray were defeated, the skirmish being nicknamed the Battle of Herrings. Thus the English soldiers who fought at Agincourt, like the seamen who fifty poor people on Maundy Thursday, he gave each twelve pence, three ells of good canvas for shirts, a pair of shoes, and a cask of red herring.

In 1563 a statute was passed containing many clauses for the encouragement of English shipping and seamen in order to support the Navy. Among its clauses is one intended to assist the herring fishery by allowing herrings and other fish caught on our coasts to be exported free of duty, and another, of far-reaching wisdom, providing that no foreign ship should carry any English goods along the coast from one English port to another.

National policy and national trade then went together.

In the famous Household Book of the Percy family the breakfast for the Earl of Northumberland and his lady consists of, among other things, a quart of beer and a quart of wine, two pieces of salt fish, six baconed herrings, four white herrings, or a dish of sprats. " Baconed herrings " are no doubt the high dried red herring; I have heard them called " ham herrings " in the Fakenham district of Norfolk, and ham-cured herrings is a description used by some London fishmongers to-day.

In 1563 Gaspar Seelar, a German, and in 1565 Francis Berty, a Frenchman, were given grants to make salt in England for the fishing industry.

Dr. John Dee in " The Petty Navy Royal "

The Herring B

ail's into Harbour.

(1577), gives 1540 as the date of the beginning of the Dutch herring fishery on the English coast, off Yarmouth. At the same date 300 foreign vessels had fished for herrings near Aberystwyth, and the Lancashire coast, and the author estimates that there were then 500 herring busses[1] resorting out of the Low Countries, under " King Philip his domain," and 100 more of French ownership. Dee assisted Robert Hitchcock, author of the " Politique Platt " (1580—91) to rouse public opinion towards building up the English Navy, which was then unable to protect either commerce, shipping, fishing, or to put down pirates, keep off spies, " Catholic traffickers," and the like, so that England was much exposed to attacks by the French, assisted by the agents of Philip of Spain and Mary, Queen of Scots. The privately-owned English vessels which warred against these foreign invaders—pirates as the Spaniards called them, privateers as we should call them now—proved excellent recruits for Drake, and later assisted him in repelling the Spanish Armada ; a petty navy born of a fishery protection force and of the herring fishery would, as Dee perceived, form a nursery for the Navy. He therefore supported Hitchcock, who had spoken in Parliament and at public dinners and had published pamphlets for the purpose of enlisting public support for

[1] In 1416 the word " busses " (latterly pronounced bushes), as applied to the vessels used by the Dutch in the herring fishery, first appeared, and was soon extended to those of other nations.

the policy of a strong Navy, and of urging the importance of the naval question to the future of England. One of the arguments put forward was that whereas the merchant adventurers of England were willing to take sporting chances in piratical adventures and in voyaging to America, where the profit was often problematical, they were stupidly blind to the certain profit and national benefit that would accrue from the English herring fishery by strengthening it so as to oust the Dutch and at the same time provide a national Navy. As regards the blind indifference of the merchant adventurers, the truth of Dee's indictment can be verified from another source.

In 1603 Sir Walter Raleigh, with whom the English fisheries were a favourite subject, laid before King James a small MS. essay called " Observations concerning the Trade and Commerce of England with the Dutch and other Foreign Nations." " The greatest fishing that ever was known in the world," he says, " is upon the coasts of England, Scotland, and Ireland, but the great fishery is in the Low Countries, and other petty States, wherewith they serve themselves and all Christendom.

1. Into four towns in the Baltic, viz., Königsberg, Elbing, Stettin, and Dantzick, there are carried and vended in a year between 30,000 and 40,000 lasts of herrings,

which, being sold but at £15 or
£16 the last, is about. . . . £620,000 0 0
And we send none thither.

2. To Denmark, Norway, Sweden,
and the ports of Riga, Revel,
Narva, and other parts of Li-
vonia, etc., above 10,000 lasts of
herring, worth 170,000 0 0
And we send none to all those
countries.

3. The Hollanders send into Russia
near 1,500 lasts of herrings, sold
at about 30/- per barrel. . . 27,000 0 0
And we send thither about 20 or
30 lasts.

4. To Staden, Hamburgh, Bremen,
and Embden, about 6,000 lasts
of fish and herrings, sold at about
£15 or £16 per last 100,000 0 0
And we none at all.

5. To Cleves and Juliers, up the
Rhine to Cologne and Frankfort
on the Maine, and so over all
Germany, near 22,000 lasts
of fish and herrings, sold at
about £20 per last (and we none)
is 440,000 0 0

6. Up the River Meuse to Maestrecht,
Liège, etc., and to Zutphen,
Deventer, Campen, Swoll, etc.,
about 7,000 lasts of herrings at
£20 per last (and we none at
all) is 140,000 0 0

7. To Guelderland, Artois, Hainault,
Brabant, Flanders, Antwerp
and up the Scheldt, all over the
Archduke's countries between

8,000 and 9,000 lasts at £18 per last (and we none at all) is . .	162,000	0	0
8. The Hollanders and others carried of all sorts of herrings to Roan (Rouen) alone in one year, besides all other parts of France, 5,000 lasts (and we not 100 lasts) is	100,000	0	0
Total sterling money . .£1,759,000		0	0

Over and above these, there is a great quantity of fish vended to the Straits. Surely the stream is necessary to be turned to the good of this kingdom, to whose sea-coasts alone God has sent these great blessings, and immense riches for us to take ; and that any Nation should carry away out of this kingdom yearly great masses of money for fish taken in our seas, and sold again by them to us, must needs be a great dishonour to our nation, and hinderance to this realm."

In 1613 an arrangement was made by which Great Yarmouth was paid 3s. 4d. per barrel for sixty barrels of white herrings, and 6s. 8d. a cask for ten casks of full red herring of " one night's death," for the use of the King's household; and in 1614 a farsighted citizen of the same town, Tobias Gentleman, by name, wrote a tract pointing out how great profit could be brought into England by the " erecting, building and adventuring of Busses to sea, a fishing." He estimates the annual value of herring caught

in English waters and sold by the Dutch herring
busses at a sum equal to £4,500,000 sterling of
our money.   He gives the names of boats other
than busses used by the Dutch for catching
herring in English waters, " Sword Pinks,
Flat-bottoms, Holland Toads, Crab-Skuits, and
Yevers." The herring caught at this time by
the Dutch were sent in large quantities to
Rochelle, Bordeaux, St. Malo, Paris and other
French towns in exchange for wine, salt,
feathers, rosin, woad, Normandy canvas, vitere
(glass), Dowlais cloth (dowlas, or coarse linen),
and French coin ; they were also exported to
Norway and Sprucia (Prussia) in exchange for
hoops and barrel boards.   Tobias Gentleman
states that the Dutch considered the profit of
the herring fishery so certain that they invested
their children's money in the fishing, even trust
funds for orphans being placed " adventuring
in the Busses." The " yagers " (fish carriers, or
ferries) purchasing the herrings from the boats
at sea, paid in ready money, or tallies, which
tallies were regarded as bills of exchange, and
were paid at sight.

The tract also deals with the excellence of the
Dutch commercial organisations, especially in
the fishing trade, and the slackness of England
in commercial matters ; it was followed up by
" Britain's Buss, or A computation as well of
the Charge of a Buss or Herring Fish Ship ;
as also of the Gain and Profit thereby, by E. S.
1615," in which will be found all particulars

needful for fowlers to call several kinds of fowls or birds to their nets or snares."

Of its practical value we have found no record.

But the reign of Charles I. is too serious a subject to introduce at the end of a chapter. To appreciate the importance of the levying of ship money in its true light as an expedient for the increase of the naval power of England against the menace of Dutch skippers, we must now turn to the history of the industry in Holland, and see by what means the Dutch had acquired their peculiar position in the herring industry.

CHAPTER III

THE HERRING FISHERY

SECTION I.—THE DUTCH FISHERY.

THE herring fishing off the coast of Scania continued till the early part of the sixteenth century, when the fish, which had failed several times in the fifteenth century, left the coast for good and frequented the Scottish coast, the Irish seas and the shores of the Low Countries. There it was that a Dutchman discovered that improved method of curing, preserving and barrelling the herring which changed the course of European history.[1] Beuckels, Beuckelzon, or Beuckelsen, was born, according to some, in 1347, according to others in 1387, and his discovery, in the opinion of so great an authority as McCulloch, contributed more than anything else to the growth of the mercantile power and wealth of Holland. The eating of butcher's meat being prohibited during two days every week, and for forty days before Lent, the new method was of the greatest importance to the whole Christian world. The Emperor Charles V. bore public witness to this

---

[1] The salted or preserved herrings to which reference is made in the early documents already quoted were merely herrings packed in or sprinkled with salt to keep the fish from decomposition. Peacock, in the "Misfortunes of Elphin," humorously describes his exiled prince as "the first Briton who caught fish on a large scale and salted them for other purposes than home consumption."

So flourishing an industry as the herring fishery was a natural temptation to neighbouring rulers, who from time to time exacted, or tried to exact, a tax on the fish taken on their coasts. In 1541, for instance, the Duke of Burgundy imposed a tax on herring at Sluys; the citizens of Ghent refused to pay, and the dispute resulted in a war in which the burghers were defeated and afterwards had to pay a heavy fine for their contumacy.

Guicciardini in his description of the Netherlands in 1560, referring to the herring fishery of the maritime provinces of Friesland (of which Groningen then formed part), Holland, Zeeland, and Flanders, states that these provinces employed about 700 vessels, each of which made three voyages in the herring season. Each vessel captured on an average 70 lasts of herrings per season; each last contained twelve barrels, of from 800 to 1,000 fish per barrel; each barrel was worth about £6 sterling; so that the value of the year's fishing in these four provinces alone was about £300,000 sterling.

In the first quarter of the seventeenth century the practice of using jag(g)ers, or " vent-jag(g)ers " [1] came into use among the Dutch for distant as well as local fisheries. The busses, being slow boats, had been obliged to sail home directly their cargo was complete, so that the

---

[1] Pronounced " yagers "; whence the word " yacht." Jager = the German jäger, hunter or courser, and ventjager = wind-racer, yacht.

The Herring

nket or Feast.

advantage of landing the herring early in the season, when fresh herrings fetched large prices, was lost. In order to secure the advantage of early markets therefore, these ventjagers (fast sailing vessels) used to accompany the Dutch herring fleet, take up the early catches of herrings, and sail with all speed to the Dutch coast. Their place to-day is taken by steam fish carriers which ferry the fish from the vessels on the fishing-grounds to the British ports.

An early reference to these jagers appears in the year 1556, but it only refers to the fisheries near the mouths of rivers. The first Dutch Law relating to the ventjagers at sea appears to be that of 1604.

The eagerness to reach markets early with the first catches of herrings is often mentioned in the records. The herrings, in ordinary circumstances, were conveyed by slow-moving waggons and canal boats, but when the first jagers arrived at the Dutch ports they were met by fast-trotting horses in light gigs, capable of carrying a few barrels of herring only. The fish were then raced to the chief markets, and to have the honour of appearing there first at the beginning of the herring season was regarded as a valuable advertisement.

On the arrival of the first herrings in Dutch cities the town crier announced the New Herring, and flags were hung out of the houses. The Festival of the Herring was to the Dutch as

the Festival of the Vineyards to the nations of
warmer climates.

SECTION II.—THE DUTCH AND ENGLISH QUESTION IN THE SEVENTEENTH CENTURY.

Dominium Maris. Throughout the history
of the Dutch herring fishery, and especially
that part which deals with the Zuider Zee
under the Republic of the United Provinces,
whether expressed or tacitly held, runs the
doctrine of the Dominion of the Seas. The
right to fish all over the open seas, and the
question of *Dominium Maris* were the cause
of endless disputes and claims by the Dutch,
and in an indirect way resemble the claims
which the Germans have advanced about
the " freedom of the seas " during the present
War. But the meaning which the Central
European Powers and the Papal Note seek in
1917 to place on the words "Freedom of the
seas " is the very opposite to that placed upon
them by Grotius.

The question was raised by Grotius in his
Mare Liberum (1608), his contention being that
the high seas were open to all. It was to counteract his influence that in 1635 at the request of
Charles I. John Selden again took up his
Mare Clausum, a work begun as early as 1618
(but at the request of James I. not published
for fear of subsequent complications with
Denmark), when Grotius was one of the Dutch

commissioners in England at a conference called
to decide the question whether an English
royal licence was required before Dutch vessels
could fish in Greenland waters. The point was
no new one. But it was the pivot upon which
turned the great decisions of International Law
and British naval policy, and on its interpretation ultimately rest the foundations of the
British Empire as we now know it.

The English claim was far more ancient
than is commonly supposed. As far back as
1295 Edward I. styled himself " sovereign of
the sea," but forbade his own subjects to
molest the Dutch, Zeelanders and Frisons while
fishing off Yarmouth, and in 1384 what may
be called the first Navigation Act was passed.
Henry VI., however, in 1440 rejected the pro-
posal of the Commons to resume the policy
embodied in this Act, 5 Richard II., c. 3.

Two Acts in the reign of Henry VII. in 1485
and 1489, an Act of Henry VIII., 1541, and an
Act of Elizabeth, 1593, all dealt with the privileges of English shipping. About the time of
the marriage of Queen Mary with King Philip
of Spain, the English claim to the sovereignty
of the seas was enforced by compelling King
Philip's subjects in Flanders to pay a fine and
an annual rent of £1,000 for a twenty-one
years' lease of the fishing near the North Irish
coast, while a similar lease with similar conditions was granted by Queen Mary to " the
Company of the old Hans." Foreign subjects

were forbidden to fish in English waters
without licences which were granted at Scarborough Castle. With the decline of the
English sea power foreigners ceased to acknowledge these claims, and the necessity for purchasing a licence was disregarded.

James I., who had a statesmanlike perception of the importance of the subject, appointed
a Commission to attend to the same matter
in 1622. Charles I. renewed certain old laws
for the benefit of English shipping, and
announced his intention of subjecting all fishing in British waters to his royal licence and
recognisance in the shape of a special tax.
By this levy, enforced in the face of protest by
the Dutch, 2s. per last for the year was exacted
from the Dutch herring fleet, which had been
found by twelve British ships of war taking
herring in British fishing ground. Next year,
fifty-seven Dutch ships of war unsuccessfully
endeavoured to prevent the levying of the tax,
but the British admiral succeeded in collecting
no less than 20,000 florins as licence money.

The claim of the Dutch to fish off our coasts
was embodied in the "Mare Liberum" of Grotius,
although that jurist had in fact never mentioned the Dutch claim to the right of fishing
upon foreign coasts, merely asserting in general
terms the principle of the freedom of the seas.
The English Government, however, as has been
stated above, thought it advisable to issue
Selden's " Mare Clausum " before coming to an

open rupture with the Dutch for the purpose of testing by force of arms the claim to the sovereignty of the " Four Seas."

The treatise, dedicated to the King, was by his command, delivered personally in open court to the barons of the Exchequer by Sir William Beecher, one of the clerks of the Privy Council, and placed among the Exchequer records, where it still remains. Selden's reasoning was based on records and precedents of the titles and claims of the Saxon and Norman kings of England. But it is only fair to remember that in early times there was little or no maritime trade or naval power in existence, except in the Mediterranean, so that the cases adduced offered no real parallel to the conditions of Selden's day, when all the nations whose territory bordered on the northern and western seas of Europe transacted a large volume of trade by sea, and in many cases maintained naval forces to protect it. Nor is it surprising that the claim of one of these powers to the dominion of the seas should attract the hostility of other nations. Charles I. at all events was determined to compel the Dutch to acknowledge this dominion, and as a preliminary built the largest ship of war that had ever been seen in England, *The Sovereign*, of 96 guns and 1,740 tons burthen. A large fleet was also necessary, and Lord Chancellor Coventry was ordered to issue writs to the sheriffs of the several counties

and to the magistrates of the several towns
" for assessing and collecting money for fitting
out ships of war, for the suppression of pirates,
and for the guard of the seas." The ships
were to be from 100 to 900 tons burthen,
manned with from 40 to 360 men to each ship,
the most general size being 500 tons, with
200 men and a commander. Each ship was to
be fitted with cannon, small arms, spears,
darts and ammunition, and maintained by its
respective county for twenty-six weeks of each
year with all provisions, equipment, and neces-
saries, together with the same amount in
reserve, the expense of a 500-ton ship and crew
for the twenty-six weeks being about £8,000.
The " ship money " was to be received by
the officers of the ships, who were further
empowered to provide and fit out from the
King's dockyards a suitable ship or ships on
behalf of the towns and counties thus assessed.
Norfolk provided one of the largest ships, a
vessel of 800 tons with a commander and 320
men, a contribution only exceeded in size by
that of Devonshire, of 900 tons and a crew of
360. The City of London provided two ships
of 800 tons and 320 men, and there were in all
forty-four ships, of a total of 11,500 tons,
manned by crews numbering 8,610. This
imposition of " ship money," therefore, cost
the country about £200,000 a year, and was
repeated annually till 1639, when the king
excused such towns and counties as by their

The larger medal was issued in 1630 to assert the claim of England to the dominion
the sea, as maintained by Selden, and in accordance with instructions given by
arles I. to his minister at the Hague: "we hold it a principle not to be denied,
t the King of Great Britain is a monarch at sea and on land to the full extent of
dominions. His Majesty finds it necessary for his own defence and safety to re-
ume and keep his ancient and undoubted rights in the Dominion of the Seas."

he smaller medal, 1662, relates to the ill feeling which existed between the
lish and Dutch soon after the Restoration. It arose from the anger felt by the
lish at the encroachment of the Dutch herring fishermen into English waters
ch led to frequent disputes; besides, the Dutch persistently refused to lower their
to ships of Great Britain in the British Seas.

situation were unable to provide the ships
with which they were charged, permitting
them to supply instead an assessed sum of
money.

Ship money was a tax formerly levied on
the maritime towns and counties in times of
war, and sometimes commuted by a money
payment. In 1628 Charles I. had extended
the principle to inland towns and counties
to secure the county against the dangers of a
French invasion, but the writs were withdrawn
in the face of violent opposition. In October,
1634, the tax was levied for the following year
in time of peace, and in 1635, as already stated,
Selden's treatise was issued to strengthen the
hands of the Government. Few people realise
the connection of ship money with the herring
fisheries, and fewer still have seen that, had
its form been constitutional, the policy of
Charles I. might have been acclaimed as the
forerunner of the great naval policy of Cromwell.

But the ships thus acquired served their
purpose, and the King, having forbidden
foreigners to fish on our coasts without his
licence, was enabled in 1636 to send a fleet
which attacked and put to flight the Dutch
fishing vessels that had infringed this order,
some of them being sunk by the English fleet;
many of the rest in a crippled state were
forced to take shelter in English harbours. The
Dutch agreed to pay Charles I. £30,000 for
permission to finish that year's fishing, and to

pay the same sum yearly for the same permission. The gain to the English was, as so
often happens, not taken full advantage of,
and in 1637—8, when the English fishermen
sent herring to Dantzig the fish were so badly
cured that considerable loss fell upon the
fishermen. De Witt, in his "Interest of
Holland," remarks when speaking of this
matter, "Whereupon the British changed
their former claim upon the whole fishery
for that of demanding The Tenth Herring,
which the diligent and frugal Hollanders considered to be a claim by the English that
the Dutch should catch herring for, and pay
tribute to a slothful and wasteful people
simply for the right of passing along the coast
of Britain."

In April, 1639, however, when Charles I. was
at York, on his way to suppress the rebellion
in Scotland, he found himself compelled to
revoke many of his previous licences, grants,
monopolies, privileges and commissions, pre-
viously issued, among them one for " gauging
red herring," while the question of ship
money was decided once for all by an Act of
Parliament (17 Car. I. c. 2), introduced by
Selden in 1641, and by the Civil War which
followed.

The dispute regarding the right of the Dutch
to fish in the " Straights " was carried on by
Cromwell, but it was soon merged in the larger
questions involved in his naval policy, which

ended in a radical change in the status of the Dutch fishery.[1]

This policy was embodied in the celebrated Navigation Act of 1651, confirmed nine years later, which gave birth to the British mercantile marine and the British Navy, and settled the predominance of British naval power. It would not be going too far to say that this Act was one of the foundation stones upon which the commercial prosperity of modern England is built. It was the abandonment of the policy for which it stood, by the repeal in 1849 of our navigation laws, that gave Germany the first weapon with which eventually to embark upon the present war by providing her with wealth with which to create her mercantile marine and overseas trade and support the navy now conducting the submarine warfare against this country. The madness which permitted this repeal has quite recently repeated itself when the Government of this country forgot that Britain is an island and endeavoured to fasten upon us the Declaration of London and the policy of a Little Navy; the valuable part played before the war by Mr. Thomas Gibson Bowles, and in a lesser degree by Lord Desborough, and the Council of the Association of Chambers of Commerce

[1] The subject is treated in detail by Beaujon in his " History of the Dutch Sea Fisheries," and briefly explained in a speech, delivered by the author of this present book before the members of the Institute of Shipbrokers, London, on February 24th, 1916, and afterwards published by the Institute as a pamphlet, under the title of " Merchant Shipping as a Weapon against Germany," by A. M. Samuel.

in London, but the enterprise, perhaps the first attempt to carry out the suggestions of the anonymous author of " Britain's Buss," was not a success.

In 1661 the Parliament of Scotland, following the English policy in matters relating to commerce, passed navigation laws for the encouragement of native shipping and navigation, as also an Act for founding companies to extend the herring and other fisheries, and granting bounties on the export of fish—a policy that was subsequently carried out on many occasions.

In the same year, Charles II. constituted the Royal Fishery Company of Great Britain and appointed the Duke of York, Lord Clarendon, and others to form a committee or council ; the project however, came to nothing, although the enterprise was more free from restrictions than the undertaking favoured by the Commonwealth Government in 1654. The new company was privileged to set up a lottery and to collect funds in all parish churches ; taverns, inns and alehouses were compelled by law to buy one barrel of herrings at 30s. per barrel and a duty of 2s. 6d. per barrel was paid to the company by persons who imported foreign-caught herring.

Two years later, by a Statute for The Farther Improvement of Former Navigation Acts, and for the Encouragement of the North Sea, etc., Fisheries, no fresh herrings were

The Hooping o

erring Barrils.

allowed to be imported into England except in English-built ships, salt for the fisheries of New England and Newfoundland being exempt from its provisions. In the same year two Acts were passed for the encouragement of the manufacture of linen and tapestry—the latter a revival of the famous Mortlake tapestry factories of James I. and Charles I., for the use of which the cartoons of Raphael had been brought to England—the encouragement of the importation of foreign manufactures and the regulation of the packing of herrings. It was also enacted that no ship should sail for Iceland from England till March 10th of each year, this provision being made to protect the fish at breeding time and the newly developed spawn.

A new Company of the Royal Fishery was incorporated in 1677, the Duke of York, the Earl of Danby, and many peers and gentlemen being partners. All the privileges enjoyed by any former Fishery Company were conferred upon this venture; it had power to purchase land, and a bounty of £20 for every dogger or buss built and fitted out was to be paid out of the Customs of the Port of London for a period of seven years. The capital was £10,980, afterwards increased to £12,580, but this was absorbed by the building of seven busses. Some of these, with their cargoes, were captured by the French, who had become very prosperous in their maritime and commercial undertakings

probably have captured the trade of red
herrings long before but for two reasons:
(1) that fish must be brought fresh to land
to be cured, as at Yarmouth, which the Dutch
could not do because the herring are found
near our own coasts, and at too great a distance
from their own; (2) that they must be smoked
with wood, a source of difficulty to the Dutch,
because Holland was not a woody country,
and high prices had to be paid for fuel.

" A Discourse of the Fishery, Briefly laying
open not only the Advantages, and Facility of
the Undertaking, but likewise the Absolute
Necessity of it, in Order to the Well-being
both of King and People," by the famous
pamphleteer Sir Roger L'Estrange, of Hun-
stanton, Norfolk, who bore the nickname
" Oliver's fiddler," 1674, deals with the riches
Holland has gained from the fisheries, to which
she owes all her greatness, and is now " taking
from his Majesties Seas no less than Ten Million
of Pounds Sterling worth " of herring, cod and
ling. L'Estrange urges that we have the advantage of situation, the fish being found upon our
coast, and our vessels not being detained by
contrary winds, but safe in their own harbours;
that the fishery, whether bringing profit or loss,
would still abundantly answer the expense;
that it is " the only Nursery of Seamen," and
therefore essential to the safety of the nation;
and that since fishermen already act as coasting
pilots, and had proved indispensable to his

Majesty's fleet in the late wars, they should be officially recognised and their functions extended [since who but they know the banks and shoals upon our coasts ?], and that this could only be by increasing their numbers and improving their condition. He refers at the end to the works of Sir Walter Rawleigh and Sir John Burrowes, and concludes by saying that he has said enough to vindicate his assertion of the " Absolute Necessity, as well as the Advantages," of such a policy.

Burroughs (Sir John), or Borough, or Burrowes (a very familiar name in Norfolk in all its variations), *d*. 1643, was one of the most distinguished students of the age. He became Keeper of the Records in the Tower of London in 1623, Norroy King-at-Arms in 1624 and in 1634, Garter King of Arms—in the latter capacity having for several years much personal intercourse with Charles I., of whom he was a devoted adherent. His " Soveraignty of the British Seas " was, like Selden's work, a counter-blast to Grotius, and shows the perception common to the Stuarts and to their wiser adherents of the necessity for a strong fleet. Burroughs' services as a note-taker were of considerable value during the Civil War when conferences were held between the rival parties, and he was happy in the moment of his death, which occurred on October 21st, 1643, before the fortunes of his Royal master had begun to wane.

"A Discourse concerning the Fishery within the British Seas And other his Majesties Dominions. London. Printed for the Company of the Royal Fishery of England, 1695," gives a bibliography of works on the subject, as follows : "Tobias Gentleman " (whose date is given as 1615); " Britain's Buss " 1615 (said to have been reprinted in 1630); " Rawleigh's Observations," 1618 ; Gerrard Malynes, A treatise called "Lex Mercatoria," ch. 47, 1636; " The Seas Magazine Opened," written by a Person of Honour, 1653 ; Captain John Smith, " The Trade of Great Britain Displayed," 1661 ; " The Royal Trade of Fishing," 1662 ; " John Keymor's Observations," made upon the Dutch Fishing, about the year 1601, 1664 ; " The Royal Fishing Revived," etc., 1670 ; " L'Estrange's Discourse " (*q.v.*), 1674 ; " A Discourse of Salt and Fishery," written by John Collins, 1682.

The " Discourse " states amongst other things that in the charter granted by Charles II. to the Royal Fisheries all fishermen were " exempt from serving on Juries, or Inquests, at Westminster, the Assizes, Sessions or Elsewhere," as well as other personal privileges. This company, however, failed, from inadequate support, says the " Discourse," which goes on nevertheless to estimate the gains of the new company at £1,000 per vessel—" One *half* whereof were sufficient gain for Encouraging the Undertaking; Yea one Quarter," with which words it ends.

During the reign of Charles II. the Dutch fishermen brought great prosperity to Yarmouth, and Mr. Secretary Coke gives us a vivid picture of an East Coast scene :—

"Whilst the fishings continue, the Dutch, with above 1,000 sail of busses, besides their jagers and other ships, victual themselves from our shore with bread, beer, flesh and butter, and dry their nets upon the land, especially in a field near Yarmouth, which is two miles in length, and they come ashore sometimes above ten thousand persons, which, besides the victualling of their ships, carry from hence to supply their country both corn, beer and beans in a very great proportion. Yarmouth alone employeth forty brewers for their service."

Perhaps because of this immigrant population Yarmouth in the seventeenth century was no peaceful place. "An Act for setling the Differences betweene the Townes of Great and Little Yarmouth[1] touching the lading and unlading of Herrings and other Merchandises and Commodityes" was passed in 1676, and again in 1677, and these Acts recite that there had

"beene heretofore many differences between the Townes of Great and Little Yarmouth, in the Countyes of Norfolke and Suffolke, or in one or both of them, to the impoverishing of both by mutuall dissentions, the mutual determination of which would tend greatly to the peace of both."

But whatever encouragement these Acts may have given to the fisheries, the naval

---

[1] Otherwise known as "Southtowne."

policy of Charles II. did English shipping
much harm. The Dutch War of 1665 was
popular, but the insult of 1667, when the Dutch
sailed up the Medway and

" An English pilot too (O shame ! O sin !)
Cheated of 's pay, was he that showed them in," [1]

caused an outburst of popular fury against
the Dutch that survived to embarrass the
sufficiently perplexing position of William of
Orange, as ruler of the two countries which
had been at each other's throats for the three
preceding decades. His closing days must have
been galled by the disaster to the Dutch
fishing fleet, when in 1702 six French men-of-
war attacked it at sea and burnt no fewer than
400 ships, after having sunk the admiral's ship
and driven off the three other Dutch ships of
war.

That singular person, James Puckle, author
of " The Club " (1667 (?)—1724) and grandson
of a Mayor of Norwich, took a prominent
part in the fishermen's question under
William III. He was the promoter of another
Royal Fishery of England Company, and in
1696 issued a pamphlet entitled " England's
Interests, or a Brief Discourse of the Royal
Fishery in a letter to a Friend," which was
altered and reissued under a new title [2] the
following year, a second time altered, enlarged
and largely re-written as " England's Way to
Wealth and Honour, in a Dialogue between an

[1] Marvell's " Last Instructions to a Painter about the Dutch Wars."
[2] For the full titles and other details see the Bibliography.

Englishman and Dutchman," also published
in 1697. A fourth version published in 1700
as " England's Path to Wealth " reached a
second edition in 1718, was translated into
Swedish five years later, and finally—proof
of its more than national interest—included
among the Somers tracts. Any one desiring
to investigate the subject of the herring industry
at the close of the seventeenth century should
turn to Puckle's curious and vivacious pages.

SECTION III.—THE ENGLISH HERRING FISHERY IN THE EIGHTEENTH CENTURY.

In 1704 Queen Anne reorganised the various
laws relating to the herring fishery. She permitted the use of all harbours and shores for
landings on payment of reasonable dues, did
away with the exaction known as " Saturday's
fishing," or " a night's fishing," and enacted
careful regulations with regard to the quality
of salt with which the fish was to be cured. A
bounty of £10 4s. per last was given on the
export of Scottish herrings, and £24 per last on
red herrings. Foreign fishermen employed
by British subjects were entitled to the same
privileges as British subjects employed by
British employers, and various materials needed
for the fitting out of fishing boats were freed
from import duty. The salt used was not,
however, to be of Scottish origin—this was only
three years before the Union—nor, on the other

hand, was the importation of English and Irish salt into Scotland permitted. That used in England was to be French Bay or Spanish salt, or "salt upon salt made of foreign salt," and the herring barrels were to be of well-seasoned maple or oak, the latter, as is well known, greatly improving the flavour of herrings, not only when used for barrels, but when burned for the smoking of high-dried herrings.

As an instance of the changing habits of the herring it is recorded that in the summer of 1730 the herring fishermen were surprised that the shoals came south two months before the usual time, particularly in the seas between England and Ireland. Great quantities were taken in July off the Clyde, and off Londonderry, and as far south as the Wexford coast. This alteration in date was not repeated in succeeding years, otherwise it might have changed not only the trade of Lewis and the Shetlands, to which stations the Scottish and Dutch fishermen resorted, but also have deflected the currents of commerce in several of the countries of North-West Europe.

In the month of June, 1738, Duncan Forbes of Culloden took John, Duke of Argyll (Jeanie Deans' Duke), to Tyree to show him that it was possible to obtain herring in this district at that time of the year. They caught 2,000 fine fat herring, and Forbes had some of them split and grilled, with pepper and salt, and others

The Packing of the

gs into the Barrils.

" nicked " and boiled in salt water[1] for the Duke's breakfast. The Duke said he had never had herring before for that meal—a point in which, as we shall see, the national habits underwent a remarkable change in the course of the century—but only for dinner and supper. He ate two herrings cooked in each way, however, and was so impressed with the possibilities of the herring as a source of excellent food that he forwarded its interests whenever possible during the few remaining years of his life. Unless the Duke's experience was very exceptional, a remarkable change must have come over Scottish habits in the next half-century, when herrings were the usual Scottish breakfast dish. In Miss Ferrier's " Marriage " (1818, but written earlier), the fashionable London beauty who, having eloped with a young Highland soldier, returns with him to the paternal seat, cries out when the Laird laid a large piece of herring on her plate : " What am I to do with this ? Do take it away, I shall faint," to which the good old aunt replies : " I declare ! Pray was it the sight or the smell of the beast that shocked you so much, my dear lady Juliana ? "

Returning to the eighteenth century we

---

[1] Fishermen near Beachy Head have told me that they consider boiling freshly caught herring in salt water the best way to bring out the full delicacy of the fish, and I have found this to be true. The salt water sharpens and improves the palate, very much as a Spanish olive, pickled in brine, improves the palate for wine and tobacco. But the Duke was not brought up on the Yarmouth bloater, or I am confident that he would have preferred one caught just after Michaelmas and grilled, to any other form of herring.—A. M. S.

find that in 1750 was published a very interesting pamphlet, one of our very few sources of illustration at this date, entitled " A Letter to a Member of Parliament concerning the Free British Fisheries," showing designs of herring boats and nets of the period ; the author complains bitterly of the poaching by the Dutch herring vessels close in shore between Yarmouth and Southwold.

Certain of the uses to which herring were put in the middle of the eighteenth century were far from obvious. In 1752 James Solas Dodd (some of whose recipes for cooking herring will be found at the end of this book) recommends their use in febrific cases and for cataplasms, and states that the oil of herrings is " of excellent service in cramps and convulsions." His recipe for making the elixir " ossium halecum " is as follows :—

" Take 10 lbs. of herring bones, dried and grossly powdered, put them in a retort, lute it, and place it in an open furnace—give it a degree of fire every two hours till no fumes are seen in the receiver. Then let all cool, and there will be an oil, a volatile salt, and a pungent volatile spirit, which put in a clean retort, and by fire unite together. Then take eight ounces of this united spirit, and put into cucurbit with two lbs. of rectified spirits of nitre, 1 lb. of diaphoretic antimony, and 4 ounces of volatile salt of tartar, distil and cohobate as often till it is perfectly united ; then add an ounce of oil of nutmeg, and half an ounce of oil of cinnamon, digest in a matrass ten days, and pour off for use, which keep in a well stopt bottle; the dose of this is from 4 to 10 drops whenever a high volatile cordial is necessary."

Dodd was, as may be guessed, something of a character. Born in 1721, he spent six years as a surgeon's mate on board a man-of-war, and having set up for himself in London in 1751, next year began as an author with his "Essay towards a Natural History of the Herring," a work written to promote the success of the industry on the lines of the Society for the Free British Fishery. He took a part in the case of Elizabeth Canning, who " whipt three female 'prentices to death and hid them in the coal-hole," turned lecturer, playright and historian, and at the age of sixty actually embarked for Russia on the strength of an adventurer's promise to make him Ambassador to the Czarina, and returned almost destitute, only to set up as lecturer and actor in Edinburgh. He died in 1804, having left behind him an MS. autobiography from which these particulars are drawn, and the reputation of being " a gentleman of amiable and entertaining manners," and a great frequenter of " disputing societies."

In 1747, according to Vernon, the Dutch still had 3,000 herring boats and 40,000 fishermen employed in the industry, a great falling off, it is true, from the 4,000 vessels and 200,000 men of 1679, but still bringing in £5,000,000 sterling per annum. Eight years later they were employing no fewer than 152 vessels off the coast of Ireland, while the Scots had only seventeen vessels employing a total of 174 men. The Dutch, in fact, called their herring fishery their " gold mine," and this fishing was carried on entirely on the coasts of Britain. It is startling to find that in 1750 1,100 British fishermen were engaged in Dutch fishing boats, and George Walker, recommending the formation of a company to promote the British fishery, suggests that the King should call home all British seamen for employment in British waters.

One writer of the period makes the useful suggestion that Parliament should employ in the herring industry the crews of ships of war discharged in consequence of peace and that 400 vessels of fifty to a hundred tons each should be provided for this purpose by the State, which was to be a partner in the undertaking.[1]

In the circumstances it is not surprising to find George II. in his speech at the opening of Parliament in 1749 making a reference to the English industry and the advantages to be derived from encouraging it. The House of Commons thereupon appointed a committee to look into the matter, and many books and

[1] There are many other pamphlets quoted by Mitchell in his masterly work on the Herring, from page 195 onwards, which should be of great value to those who are turning their attention to the development of this country's resources, and more especially to British fisheries.

pamphlets were written dealing with the
various plans suggested, bitter complaints being
made of the salt restrictions imposed by the
Act of 1704 which hampered the progress of
the fisheries. We shall hear more of these
restrictions when we come to the public-
spirited appeals of Lord Dundonald.

The attention of the House of Commons
being thus directed to the subject, a body
of London merchants proposed to form a
joint-stock company with a capital of £500,000
provided the Government would guarantee interest at 4 per cent. on the capital. Pamphlets
were published advocating that an attempt
should be made by Great Britain to win the
herring fishery from the Dutch, an Act being
actually passed with this object. A bounty
was granted spread over a certain number of
years and payable to British fishing vessels
built in and sailing from any British port and
carrying British crews : such vessels were to
meet at the Shetlands on or before June 11th
in each year, but were not to shoot their nets
or wet them before June 13th. They were to
continue fishing, following the herrings south
till October 1st, or they might meet at Campbeltown in Argyllshire on September 1st,
and might continue fishing till December 31st.
A journal was to be kept of their proceedings,
with a record of the quantities of fish sent to
foreign markets in tenders before the vessels
came to port and of the numbers of fish brought

into British ports. Each vessel was to carry twelve Winchester bushels of salt for every last of herrings the vessel was capable of holding ; the barrels for the fish were to be new, and each vessel of 70 tons was to have two fleets of nets. There were various other provisions as to the interest on the capital subscribed for the venture, which capital might be provided under the name of a fishing chamber of a city or port. The Royal Charter of Incorporation was granted on October 11th, 1750.

The scheme did not succeed commercially. The gear and vessels were bought at very expensive rates, more people were employed than necessary, and more fish caught than could be sold either in this country or abroad in competition with the better cured herrings in the established markets of the Dutch.

Oliver Goldsmith in his essay " On the Instability of Worldly Grandeur," 1759 (*The Bee*), refers to the British White Herring Fishery Company. He says : " A few years ago the herring fishery employed all Grub Street ; it was the topic in every coffee-house, and the burden of every ballad. We were to drag up oceans of gold from the bottom of the sea ; we were to supply all Europe with herrings upon our own terms. At present we hear no more of this. We have fished up very little gold that I can learn ; nor do we furnish the world with herrings as was expected. Let us wait but a few years longer, and we shall

The Mending or Repair

the Broken Herring Netts.

find all our expectations a herring fishery."
The secretary and laureate of the company
was John Lockman, known then as the "Herring Poet." In Hogarth's "Beer Street,"
1751, the fishwomen are shown singing one of
Lockman's ballads on the herring fishery.
The ballad was then exceedingly popular at
Vauxhall Gardens. The "Herring Poet"
translated many French works, among them
the "Henriade."

By Acts of 1750, 1753, 1755, the Government paid a bounty of 3 per cent. on capital
subscribed by the Society of Free British
Fisheries, but the restrictions as to the modes
of using salt and the kinds of salt continued
to be a source of difficulty.

A supplemental Act in 1753 varied the
amount of the bounty, but permitted vessels
to put in to any port in Great Britain or
Ireland, between the interval of the Shetland
and the Yarmouth fishing, in order to prepare
for the latter. The fleets of nets might be of
any depth not under five fathoms, but the
rendezvous was changed to Kirkwall in the
Orkneys, Bressy, Bressay, Brassey or Bressa
Sound, now Lerwick Harbour, being often
mentioned about this date.

In October, 1771, a bounty of 30s. a ton for
seven years was granted to all decked vessels
of from 20 to 80 tons of British origin and
ownership engaged in the herring fishery. The
Statute appointed that the vessels should meet

for fishing at Yarmouth, Leith, Inverness, Brassey Sound, Kirkwall, Oban, Campbell-town and Whitehaven, and the bounty in Scotland was no longer to be dependent upon the production of a particular fund, but to be paid punctually from the whole revenue of the kingdom.

In 1771, although a bounty on the herring fishing was paid in the ports of England, it was stopped in Scotland. Only nineteen busses were fitted out in Scotland in 1770, and in 1771 only four, as against 263 in 1767. The Scottish fishery was thus abandoned to foreigners, who caught large quantities of herrings on the coasts of Scotland and exported them to our own West India Islands as food for the slaves.

Boswell in 1773 perceived the need of "encouragement of men to fisheries and manufactures" in order to introduce a circulation of money, since the absence of small change gave rise to serious inconveniences ("Tour," September 24th, 1773). The theory of Government bounties on the number of herring taken was fundamentally sound; though the bounties were gradually reduced, the system continued in full force till 1821, ultimately ceasing altogether in 1829. But bounties based on tonnage were unsound. "The herring vessels," in the words of one writer on economics, "went to sea to catch the bounty, and not the fish." From 1829 to 1851 the fisheries were unsupported by State encouragement. They were, however, no longer hampered by restrictive regulations, though it was only by the Sea Fisheries Act of 1868 that the Scottish herring fishery was entirely freed of restrictions.

A shrewd observation has been made that all the fisheries that have ever prospered have risen gradually from small beginnings, the number of people bred to them, and the increase of markets keeping pace with the gradual increase in the quantity of fish caught, thus avoiding the waste and want of thrifty management always associated with the peculiar methods and loose organisation of an enterprise carried on by joint-stock companies or administered under State control, even though the undertaking be a monopoly.

The hand of the State being removed, we see from the Report on the Herring Fisheries of Scotland by Buckland, Walpole and Young (1878), that the history of the industry from 1809 onwards, though marked by constant fluctuations from year to year, is, on the whole, a record of continual prosperity. The improvement is the more noteworthy because in the course of a century the export trade in herrings has undergone many revolutions. The Irish demand has decreased, and with the abolition of slavery the export of herring to the West Indies has almost entirely ceased. Steamboats and railways, however, have had an extremely beneficial effect as increasing the area of distribution, though, as already said, there is room for improvement in this respect.

In the year 1773 we see the Scottish herring fleet in illustrious company. It was in the autumn of that year that Dr. Johnson " was induced to undertake the journey," as he himself says, " by finding in Mr. Boswell a companion, whose acuteness would help my inquiry, and whose gaiety of conversation and civility of manners are sufficient to counteract the inconveniences of travel, in countries less hospitable than we have passed." Unfortunately, in spite of their joint eulogiums upon Scottish breakfasts, neither Johnson nor Boswell particularises herring, probably because it was too familiar, though smoked salmon is mentioned, but on Sunday, October 3rd, they got the first hint of a change of wind from " a little fleet of herring-busses passing by for Mull," and therefore left Skye for the Sound of Mull ; their vessel " kept near the five herring vessels for some time," but, the wind changing, they were obliged to tack, and finally run for Col.

To Johnson's eulogium already mentioned, " if an epicure could remove by a wish, in quest of sensual gratifications, wherever he had supped, he would breakfast in Scotland," we may adduce a parallel from a quarter at least equally impartial. Peacock, who hated the Scots as he hated nothing but Lord Brougham—and like Johnson he was a good hater—makes Mr. MacQuedy say in "Crotchet Castle," in a discussion on breakfasts :—

"Well, Sir, and what say you to a fine fresh trout, hot and dry, in a napkin, or a herring out of the water into the frying-pan, on the shore of Loch Fyne ? "

to which the Reverend Dr. Folliott classically and characteristically replies :—

"Sir, I say every nation has some eximious virtue ; and your country is pre-eminent in the glory of fish for breakfast."

Going back to the reign of George II. from which the question of bounties led us to violate chronology, we find in the Dutch herring industry of 1750 a melancholy contrast to the English. Ever on the look-out to improve their processes, the Dutch made even stricter regulations concerning the quality of salt to be used for herrings, no Spanish or Portugal salt being permitted in herring casks before the curing master had examined it. Only Spanish or Portugal salt was to be taken to sea for the herring fishing by the vessels of Holland and West Friesland, the use of French salt from St. Martins, Olderdame, the South of France, the West Indies, and other places being prohibited under pain of forfeiture of the catch. After St. James's Day and Bartholomew-tide, however, the fishermen were allowed to salt the fish with fresh salt, boiled with sea water, according to agreement with the City of Cologne.[1]

[1] *Cf*. pp. 103 and 146.

Herring caught at the beginning of the season made large prices.   In 1763 two barrels containing 1,600 herring were sold in Shetland at 570 guilders (£52 sterling) per barrel, and 12¾ barrels were sold at 460 guilders (£42 sterling) per barrel, making a total of £639 for 12,000 fish, or over a shilling per fish. (See Macpherson's " Annals of Commerce," Vol. III. p. 373.)

But the Dutch were not our only rivals. During the years 1764—5 the Swedes exported from Gothenberg 20,000 barrels of herrings to Ireland, whence they were carried to the British Colonies, which also received a great quantity from the Dutch and Danes by clandestine trade from the Islands of St. Eustathius and Santa Cruz.   The years 1770—80 were also successful years for the Swedish fisheries.   In one year alone 800,000,000 herrings were boiled down for the purpose of producing oil, the yield being 1,250,000 gallons.   It is plain that Thomson's protest had lost none of its force, when he exhorted the British seamen of George II.'s reign to learn

> " with adventurous oar
> How to dash wide the billow : nor look on,
> Shamefully passive, while Batavia's fleet
> Defrauds us of the glittering finny swarms
> That heave our firths, and crowd upon our shores ;
> How all enlivening trades to rouse, and wing
> The prosperous sail, from every growing port,
> Unchallenged, round the sea-encircled globe,
> And thus in soul united as in name,
> Bid Britain reign the mistress of the deep."

During the year 1764 the movements of the herring were very capricious.   They deserted the coasts of Sweden, but on the west coasts of Ireland and Scotland, in the words of a writer at the time, " the abundance of these heaven-directed visitors was inconceivably great," Irish fishermen being able to load their boats with a single haul of the nets. Three months of the summer fishing yielded £54 per boat, although the price realised by the herring was exceedingly low, about 10d. per 1,000 during the month of July ; the weight of 1,000 herring would be over 3 cwts., the weight of two stoutly built men, or more than an average horse can conveniently carry on its back. Millions of fish were boiled down for oil for currying leather, and millions were thrown away. In seven or eight weeks so many herrings were caught in Loch Hourn that if they could have been brought to market, they would, at the ruling price, have realised £56,000. The captures made during these seven or eight weeks were so great that the stock of salt and casks in the district was entirely exhausted, and fishermen gave up catching any more herring in Loch Hourn, as they were apparently ignorant of how to make oil from the herring, or were unable to extract the oil owing to the lack of fuel. The herring fishing in this part of Inverness was carried on with little knowledge and foresight, and, although the lochs were well stored with herring, the fisher-folk were unable in most years to turn their captures to reasonable commercial profit. The loch was again visited by large shoals of herring during the year 1767 and 1768, while in 1782 the pressure of the shoals was so great that those nearest the open sea drove many millions of herrings on to the beaches along with other fish of various kinds and larger sizes.

The influence of successful fishing seasons on population may be very marked. In the *Times* of March 28th, 1871, appears a notice connecting herrings and marriages, in which the registrar of Fraserburgh stated that the herring fishery was very successful for the third quarter of the year, and that consequently marriages were 80 per cent. above the average. On the other hand, the registrar of Tarbert reported a bad fishing season for the same quarter, with the result that there was not a single wedding solemnised in his parish, while the registrar of Lochgilphead also stated that the herring fishery was a failure to the loch, and no marriages were solemnised during that quarter. A bad fishing, therefore, may mean no marriages in the fishing villages.

In 1767 the King of Denmark established a herring fishery company at Altona with the intention of fishing the coasts of Shetland and Scotland, whereupon the Society of Free British Fisheries asked that British ships of war should protect the British fishermen from the encroachments of foreigners on the fishing grounds off our coasts, and requested our minister at Hamburg to prevent Dutch herrings

being imported there on easier terms than
British, on the ground that it was contrary
to the treaty made by the British society with
the magistrates of Hamburg relating to the
importation of British herrings.

About the year 1770 fishermen from the
Norfolk and Suffolk coasts, and especially
those of Harwich, complained that the restrictions and duties upon salt frequently obliged
them to throw away their catches of fish
instead of curing them; the Coast Office
charges at London were also a cause of trouble.
The Dutch competed with the English East
Coast fishermen in the supply of the London
market, which by long experience they had
attained the art of feeding with such exactness
that they were able to keep up a constant and
exorbitant price against the consumers.

A similar charge has often been brought,
even in recent years, against the British fishing
industry. Not long ago it was stated that in
order to maintain prices when very large
numbers of herring had been caught and
brought into port, the fish were intentionally
allowed to spoil and then sold as manure.
Gluts of fish, and especially herrings, are unex-
pectedly yielded by the sea from time to time,
and it is at such times that the State should
step in to secure the uncured fish for rapid
transportation in cold storage and distribution
as food in remote inland parts of these islands,
after treatment by the brine-freezing process.

Premiums were paid in the City of London
in 1772 for bringing herring and mackerel to
market, and large quantities were attracted to
Billingsgate, but only in the course of the
autumn season, the competition bringing down
the market price of butcher's meat appreciably.
Yet in 1775, 341 of the 768 trading vessels
which arrived at Hamburg during the year
came with cargoes of herring from Shetland,
and of these twenty-eight were Danish, two
Prussian, two Dutch, and none British.

Great quantities of herrings were normally
exported to the West Indies. 23,000 barrels
went from Greenock alone during 1777—8, each
barrel measuring 31½ gallons and containing
from 700 to 900 herrings. In the year 1777
there were nine houses for the smoking of red
herring at Dunbar, in which a million and a
quarter fish could be smoked at once.

In 1776, owing to the American War, which
had an adverse effect upon the British herring
fishery, the rate of insurance on homeward-
bound ships from the West Indies rose to
23 per cent. At the outbreak of the French
War, however, the rate actually rose to 50 per
cent. as against 3 per cent. on the marine
risks in peace time.

In 1776 the export of salted provisions from Ireland was also prohibited lest the French should
obtain Irish provisions for victualling their fleet
in the impending war. This embargo had a
further adverse effect upon the herring industry.

Between the years 1777—81 the average consumption per annum of red herrings in England was roughly 13,000,000, the average annual consumption of white herrings about 5,000 barrels, each containing about 800 fish.

In 1779 it was estimated that two-thirds of the seamen who manned the shipping of the Clyde, besides a considerable number in the vessels belonging to Liverpool, Bristol and London, and a great number in the Navy, had been bred in the herring industry.

There is a connection between Lowestoft china and the herring fishery. In Chaffers's "Marks and Monograms on Pottery, etc." (1897), it is stated that Philip Walker, proprietor of the Lowestoft Porcelain Works, founded in 1756, "like many others of the gentry, had a boat, which was occasionally engaged in the mackerel and herring fisheries, from 1770 down to the year 1790. . . ." Obed Aldred, another partner, was a member of the firm of Stannard and Aldred, who "had boats engaged in the herring trade from 1769 to 1778, when they seem to have dissolved partnership."

John Richman, another partner, "was an extensive merchant, and employed several boats in the herring-fishery; in 1748 he had four, and more or less up to 1756, when he seems to have discontinued the trade, and probably devoted himself to the interests of the (Lowestoft) porcelain manufactory."

Section IV.—The Question of Preservatives.

Ice was not used generally in England as a preservative for keeping uncured fish in a fresh state till 1780, a Scotsman named Dempster being the first to use it for preserving salmon. Its use for packing fresh herrings enables the fish to be converted into bloaters in inland towns, as well as at sea-ports, and thereby greatly enlarges the area in which the preservation of fish can be carried on. Before the eighteenth century the salt question had been a subject for pamphlets and discussion, but the question became a national one when in the year 1784 Lord Dundonald published a pamphlet on the manufacture of salt and its relation to the herring industry. He complained of the little attention paid in Britain to the purity of the salt used—though the regulations, as we have seen, were strict—and of the slipshod way in which the fish were caught and cured. Even now the manner in which herrings in their various forms are offered to the public leaves much to be desired, and, without the fish being unfit for human food, the varieties of qualities and conditions are so marked that the general public is probably hindered from purchasing herrings as freely as is to be wished. Much, however, could be done by insisting that every box of bloaters should be marked with the date of catch, and by educating the public to refuse a bloater offered for sale more than seven days from the time it left the sea. A bloater bought in London is inevitably a different and inferior article compared with a bloater obtained near Yarmouth or Lowestoft, and it is a fact that in whatever way a herring is to be cured it is of the utmost importance that it should be treated immediately after capture, the delay even of a few hours spoiling its quality, and, indeed, its value as wholesome food.

But cold storage, or brine freezing, may eventually solve all difficulties. The practice of "fortifying" a bloater by increase of the smoking treatment should be discouraged, because although it gives a few days' longer life for travel and sale, it destroys the quality and delicacy of the fish. The question of the salt used in "rousing," "roosing" or sprinkling is of equal importance. Salt produced by boiling or evaporation does not leave pure preservative salt, or muriate of soda, while our common salt is composed not only of muriate of soda or pure salt, but of sulphate of magnesia (Epsom salts), muriate of magnesia, muriate of lime, and sulphate of lime—all these, except the first, being actively injurious to the process of curing. The muriate of magnesia is partly detached from common salt in a liquid state, and, from the liquid, bittern, from which magnesia is made, is formed ; a good portion, however, remains with the other injurious ingredients, after boiling or evapora-

T.H. K

tion. This trouble had not been properly dealt with in Britain, whereas the Dutch, who learnt the secret at Cologne, could produce salt of much better quality and purity than the English. Their method was to melt rock salt in pure sea water, taking care to obtain the latter at a great distance from the shore, and in this simple process lay not only the success of the Dutch cured herring, but of Dutch butter also. In modern times, however, chemists have invented processes for the production of British salt of greater purity. This salt has completely superseded Spanish and other salts used by the earlier curers in preference to British salt made by boiling and evaporation.

The analysis of the best " fishery salt " used at the present day is as follows :—

	Per cent.
Chloride of sodium and moisture .	98·99
Sulphate of lime	·51
Calcium chloride	·28
Magnesium chloride . . .	·12
Insoluble matter	·10
	100·00

A curious passage on the English salt industry in the sixteenth century will be found in " Brittain's Bulwarke of defence against all Sicknes, Sornes, and Woundes, that do daily assaulte mankinde. . . . Doen by Williyam Bulleyn, and ended this Marche, Anno Salutis 1562." On folio lxxv of the "Booke of Simples," with which the work begins, we read :—

" Much salt is made in England, . . . in Holland, in Lincolneshere, and onely by a maruelous humer of water, at the Witch (Northwich) far from the sea, and in the North there is salt made at the Shiles (Shields) by Tinmouth Castle. I Bullein the author hereof, haue a pan of salte upon the same water. At Blith in Northumberland is good salte made, and also at sir Jhon Delauals Panes, which syr Jhon Delauall Knight hath been a patron of worship, and hospitalite, most like a famous gentilman, during many yeres, and powdreth no man by the salt, of extorcion, or oppressing his neighbour, but liberally spendeth, his Salte, Wheate, and his Maulte."

When we return to our historical survey and recall the complaints as to salt duties and restrictions which hampered the industry on every side, we may marvel at the success which the herring fishery managed to attain. The first tax on salt and certain other commodities— *i.e.*, the first excise or inland duty on goods— was levied not by the Stuarts, but by the Parliament of 1643. As in modern Italy, it proved too valuable a source of revenue to be given up, since owing to the extensive salting of meat and fish for use, especially in winter and at sea, the amount of salt used per head of the population was very large.

The number of bushels of salt used in England in the year 1784, the year of Lord Dundonald's first pamphlet, " Thoughts on the Manufacture and Trade of Salt, the Herring Fisheries, etc.," was 4,200,000, yielding an annual revenue of £700,000, at 3s. 4d. per bushel duty. The down in pans with coal from Newcastle and Sunderland, which coal was liable to a duty of 5s. 4$\frac{7}{10}$d. per chalder; Limmington salt therefore paid double duty, first on the coal, then on the salt. At Liverpool rock salt was dissolved in sea water, making therewith the strongest possible brine. The importation of salt from Northwich in Cheshire (Norwich, as Lord Dundonald calls it) was only permitted in the case of the ports of England and Wales, in Swansea, Holyhead, Lawnmarsh, and such places as were within ten miles of the salt pans ; elsewhere its use was prohibited, but it could be exported duty free to Ireland whither coal could be exported at the moderate duty of 1s. 1$\frac{4}{10}$d. per chalder. The favourable position of Ireland thus enabled her to supply three-quarters of the west coast of Scotland with smuggled salt, and this preferential treatment is further illustrated by the fact that Irish fishermen were exempt from many of the restrictions imposed upon British fishermen. They could load their boats as they liked, either by capturing the herring, or by purchasing them from other fishermen. The Irish Parliament granted a bounty on the salt used for the herring fishery between June, 1784, and June, 1785, and encouraged the capture of herring by giving bounties to industries which were branches of the herring fishing, and by imposing a duty of 4s. per barrel on imported Swedish herring in 1777, the duty being

raised to 10s. per barrel in 1785 ; this high rate
of duty, however, produced much smuggling,
a trade popular and profitable even under a
Home Rule Parliament.

The English regulations on the use of salt
were already strict, but in 1784, to prevent fraud
in its use for curing fish, it was made illegal
to use foul salt as manure, and fish curers were
forbidden to deal in salt. Several alterations
were also made in the fishing laws : the herring
vessels were excused from making a super-
fluous voyage for the purpose of assembling
at a given spot preparatory to dispersal for
the fishery, but might proceed direct to the
fishing at any date between June and October ;
they were also permitted to use the salt shipped
for curing herrings for the curing of other fish,
but were not allowed any bounty on their
export ; and any fishing boat might purchase
fresh herrings from any British-owned vessel,
and might put their herring on such vessels to
get them to market at the earliest possible
moment.

Next year another Act (25 Geo. III., c. 65)
imposed a great number of restrictions on the
use of salt except for purposes of fishing, but
even then the salt was so heavily taxed that
it was cheaper to throw the fish into the sea
than to salt and sell the herring.[1]

[1] Report of the Commission appointed to inquire into the State
of the British Fisheries ; and into the most effectual Means for
their Improvement and Extension. Reported by Henry Beaufoy,
Esq., 11th May, 1785.

of heavy customs duties. The Dutch herring trade dwindled therefore, till in 1828 the Amsterdam herring trade presented a petition to the King asking that an order should be issued calculated to create a close monopoly for the sale of the Dutch product, and that the whole of the fishery should be formed into one association worked by a committee with power to fix a minimum price and to regulate sales so as to maintain that price—a trust, in short, of the strictest kind.[1]

Lord Dundonald's first pamphlet, which is not even mentioned in the account of him in the " Dictionary of National Biography," was a timely one. In the year of its publication an account by Dr. Anderson, who had been appointed by the Lords of the Treasury to make a report of the herring fisheries on the West Coast of Scotland, was laid before a Committee of the House of Commons [2] setting forth the number of foreign vessels and men employed in the herring fishery of Scotland during the summer of 1784, the full text being subsequently published as " An Account of the Present State of the Hebrides and Western Coasts of Scotland." His figures as to the number of boats employed are as follows :—

---

[1] There is one particular point in the Dutch herring regulations which is worthy of notice with regard to the gutting of the herrings. The gills, liver and stomach were the only parts to be taken away, and this was done with the finger and thumb, and not with a knife.

[2] Three similar Reports were issued in 1785, one in 1786, another in 1798, which are full of curious and interesting information. They may be consulted at the British Museum.

Deep Water, Shore, Si

d other Red-herrings.

From various parts of Holland	.	166 vessels carrying	2,265 men.
Do.	Emden (Prussian) .	44	do.	616 do.
Do.	Hamburg and Altona	29	do.	406 do.
Do.	Dunkirk . . .	7	do.	70 do.
Do.	Ostend and Newport			
	(Flanders) . .	24	do.	312 do.
The Danes had also	. . .	3 yaggers carrying	24 do.
And the Dutch	. . . .	2 store ships do.	72 do.

275 vessels carrying 3,765 men.

These vessels assembled in Brassa Sound in Shetland (Lerwick Harbour), paying nothing for anchorage ground, or for the liberty of fishing on the British coasts.

The subject of the fisheries was brought prominently into public notice during the following year, when the winter herring did not appear on the north-west coast of Ireland till December 30th, instead of in the middle of October. They remained only a few days, yet in the course of a fortnight 300 Irish boats, assisted by 400 boats from other parts of Great Britain, captured great cargoes of herring, and sold the fish at high prices, owing to the failure of the winter herrings on the coasts of Scotland and the total failure of the fishing off the coast of Sweden.

An earlier Act, by which the Highlanders of the western coast were forbidden to sell their herrings to fishing vessels, had imposed upon them a grave injustice, and tended to the depopulation and ruin of the villages at the heads of salt water lochs. This grievance was now redressed, and the liberty to sell their catches, when and where they could, conferred a great blessing upon the Highlands. Unable, owing to the character of the country in which they lived, to engage in agricultural pursuits, they depended on their fishing, but could not cure the fish for want of salt, casks and a market within reasonable distance.

The new Act " for the more effectual encouragement of the British fisheries " (1786) offered an annual bounty of 20s. per ton, to continue for seven years after June 1st, 1787, to every decked vessel of 15 tons burthen, or more, built in Great Britain after January 1st, 1780, and carrying five men for every 15 tons burthen, and one man for every 5 tons above that weight. Every such ship was also to have on board 12 bushels of salt for every last of herrings she was capable of carrying, and as many new barrels made of staves half an inch in thickness, and full bound, as she could stow; also 250 square yards of net (of any dimension most convenient), with proper appendages, for every ton of her burthen; she must sail between June 1st and October 1st direct to the fishing station and there continue fishing for three months, reckoning from the day of wetting the nets, unless she shall have sooner obtained a full cargo, wholly caught by her crew.

A further bounty of 4s. for every barrel of repacked herrings landed at the port of arrival was allowed in the proportion of two barrels and a half for every ton of the vessel's burthen, and of 1s. for every barrel beyond that proportion, the barrels to be counted at landing,

when they were in the condition of sea-steeks
(herrings salted and barrelled at sea), and
four barrels in that condition were reckoned
for three barrels of repacked. As some
encouragement to the boat fishery a bounty
of 1*s.* per barrel was allowed for herrings
properly salted and cured, landed from open
boats. All casks entitled to bounty were to
have a distinguishing mark, and also the curers'
name, branded upon them on penalty of forfeiture. The Act, however, did little. An
official account given in to the Committee of
the House of Commons in 1798 shows that in
1787 one vessel of 27 tons, belonging to Ilfra-
combe, received a bounty of £27 in virtue of
this Act, no other vessel belonging to England,
and not one vessel belonging to Scotland,
having ever received anything at all. Yet for
the further encouragement of the deep-sea
fishery on the north and north-east coasts of
this kingdom, premiums of 80, 60, 40, and
20 guineas were allotted, in addition to the
tonnage and barrel bounties, to the four
vessels having the greatest quantities of herrings caught by their own crews landed between
June 1st and the last day of November in each
of the seven years. Further, in order to extend
the sale of fish and to provide a cheap and
wholesome article of food, the duties, hitherto
payable on the carriage of fish caught by
British subjects for home consumption, were
now abolished, except in the case of fish carried

from Scotland to England, on which a duty to
equalise the salt duties was made payable.
The bounty of 5s. per ton, given by an Act
of 5 Geo. I., on particular kinds of cured fish,
was, however, reduced to 3s. Some efforts
were made by this Act to lighten the intoler-
able grievances of the salt bonds, and the
revenue officers were prohibited from taking
any fees. The bounty of 1s. per barrel was
allowed on herrings caught by boats on the
coast of Man and landed on that island ; and
the duties on the importation of herrings
thence to Great Britain were repealed.

In the same year the British Society for
Extending the Fisheries and Improving the
Sea Coasts of this Kingdom was incorporated
as a joint-stock company with shares at £50
each. The purpose of the enterprise was to
found villages, harbours, and fishing stations
on the Highlands and Islands of North Britain
for the development of fishing, agriculture and
manufactures in that part of the kingdom. It
was hoped that these villages would serve as
nurseries for seamen for the defence of the
kingdom, and so reduce the necessity for
emigration.

In 1787 there was a further extension and
modification of the Act of 1786, dealing for
the most part with the circumstances in which
bounties were to be paid. In the reports
presented to the Committee of the House of
Commons during the ten years 1787—96 it

appears that these amounted to £17,904 10s. 6d., a great contrast to the £27 earned by one fishing boat under the Act of 1786. The money was received by 251 herring boats belonging to Yarmouth, forty-two belonging to Deal, Dover, Rye and Southwold. None of the Scottish boats received the bounty, as they were built in such a way that it was impossible for them to conform with the stipulation that they should stow the six barrels of cured herrings per ton burthen which entitled them to the bounty. Further, the Scottish boats went on much longer voyages than the English, so that much of their hold space had to be filled with provisions; they also carried more boats than was usual with the English vessels, and their owners not unnaturally complained that the bounty, as far as they were concerned, was only waste paper.

In 1787 an association of Yarmouth traders fitted out herring vessels to work under the Act of 1786. Their boats proceeded to Shetland, going so far north that they were hampered with floating ice. They abandoned the usual method of shooting their nets in the lochs and bays, and tried deep water instead, the fish so caught being of excellent quality. They found a ready market and good prices at Hamburg, where they arrived before the early Dutch herrings, and even at Rotterdam. The working expenses of the undertaking, however, and the unsatisfactory way in which the English

Government paid the bounty, rendered the enterprise unprofitable, and it was given up.

In 1795 there were further modifications of the Acts of 1786 and 1787. Inhabitants of the United Provinces who had been employed in catching herrings were allowed to bring their catches into any British port free of duty, and to receive bounties on the export of such fish, on taking the Oath of Allegiance to the King of England, Dutch fishermen being invited to bring their vessels, nets and furniture into England free of charge and to become freeholders of land. Many Dutch fishermen were then prisoners of war in this country, but the hardships of the salt laws, and the want of communication between the fishing villages and the more cultivated parts of North Britain, discouraged them from availing themselves of the inducements offered by the British Government.

In 1799 the British Society for the Encouragement of the Herring Fisheries was empowered to give premiums to persons distinguishing themselves by catching and curing the fish, or in making soap and oil of those that could not be used for food—and they could be reckoned by the million. So great indeed was the number caught around the south-east coast of Scotland at the beginning of the nineteenth century that, although the failure of the Swedish industry led to a corresponding importation of Scottish herrings into

Scandinavia, numbers had to be boiled down
for the oil they contained, and a process was
invented by which herring and other fish, even
in a putrid state, provided materials which,
with turpentine, were manufactured into soap.

During the closing years of the eighteenth
century and the opening years of the nineteenth
this abundance of herring, especially along the
northern shores of the Firth of Forth, gave a
special advantage to the Fife fishermen in the
wide part of the firth. Houses were built in
the neighbourhood for curing red herring, and
large quantities of salt, and numbers of barrels
were collected. A fishing fleet drawn from all
parts of England, Scotland and Ireland
assembled in the firth to a total of 360 vessels
and 1,200 boats, and the shores were covered
with numbers of persons engaged in gutting,
salting and barrelling the fish, the scene bearing a strong resemblance to that presented
by the south coast of Sweden during the
prosperous times of the herring fishing there
several hundred years earlier.

In the year 1800 the price of bread was very
high, as will be seen from the prices ruling at
that time :—

	s.	d.	
Wheat	118	3	per quarter
Rye	79	9	,,
Barley	67	0	,,
Oats	86	6	,,
Beans	62	8	,,
Peas	67	8	,,

The revival of the herring fishery, which produced 500,000 barrels of herrings annually, therefore provided an invaluable supply of cheap and wholesome food at a time when the price of bread was exorbitant. Not only was the south of Scotland supplied, but fast sailing smacks from Berwick carried fresh herring to the London market, some packed in ice and some salted. It was found in London that the latter, when the salt had been washed away from them, were perfectly fresh, and of a quality equal to those usually sold in London, though inferior to those of Loch Fyne and some other parts of the west coast of Scotland. Great quantities of these herring, as well as red herrings, were exported to the West Indies for the use of the plantation negroes, and Stornoway herrings sold in Hamburg at £2 per barrel, while those carried to Hamburg and cured in the Dutch manner actually sold for £5 per barrel. Herrings from Leith, however, only fetched about one-third of that price owing to the inferior methods of curing practised on the east coast of Scotland.

An attempt to develop British fisheries was made by the Society of Arts. In 1805 a reward was offered for "curing herrings by the Dutch method." For some years this does not seem to have had much result, but in 1819 and 1820 two rewards of fifty guineas and £50 respectively were paid to J. F. Denovan, of Leith, for his success in the "curing of British herrings," and for introducing them into the market. Two communications in the "Transactions" (1819 and 1820) give an interesting account of the way in which, after many unsuccessful attempts to get hold of the secrets of the business in Holland, he secured the assistance of six experienced Dutch fish-curers, and with their help started to catch and cure herrings on the west coast of Scotland. After a good deal of trouble and various misadventures, he was quite successful in his enterprise, and succeeded in sending to Edinburgh and London cargoes of herrings equal to the best Dutch. The method employed, then as now, was merely, after gutting and cleaning the fish, to pack them in barrels with salt or brine. Many other awards followed, and this was the beginning of the Scottish cured-herring trade, which developed into an important business, and has, of quite recent years, spread to the East Anglian fishing ports. At the present time it is a thriving industry at Lowestoft.

This inquiry is referred to in the well-known chapter on the work of the Society of Arts in the "Microcosm of London" (1808): "The attentions of the Society have been lately directed to the best method of preventing salted provisions from becoming rancid or rusty, to the refining of fish oils, and to other valuable enquiries such as the discovery of a harmless white paint, the use of leadless glaze, and the manufacture of an indelible ink."

We may fitly close this chapter with the note that the eighteenth century witnessed the extinction after nearly 800 years of the Yarmouth Herring Fair, which lasted from Michaelmas to Martinmas, and caused infinite troubles and disputes, but which emphasised the position of the town as the head of the English herring trade in the eyes of the world.

The Selling

e Herring.

CHAPTER IV

THE HERRING INDUSTRY IN THE NINETEENTH AND TWENTIETH CENTURIES

SECTION I.—THE NINETEENTH CENTURY.

THE history of the herring fishery in the nineteenth century was, comparatively speaking, uneventful. We have already noticed the cessation of the Government bounties. The chief external events in the fishing world were the Conventions by which the rights of the States of Europe over their territorial waters were defined, those with France in 1839 and 1867, and that with the North Sea Powers, Germany, France, Belgium, Denmark and the Netherlands of 1882. The first of these was brought about by the constant quarrels of French and English fishermen over the rights of the English to dredge for oysters off the French coast, and those of the French fishing fleets from Calais, Boulogne and Dieppe to fish off the coasts of Kent and Essex. The findings of the Commission of both nations appointed in 1837 were embodied in the Convention of 1839 and in an Act of Parliament in 1843, but the Convention of 1867 was required to settle the question.

The Conference of the North Sea Powers held at the Hague in 1881 was " not so much to protect the fisheries as to protect the fishermen from one another—in short, to regulate the police of the fisheries in the North Sea outside territorial waters,"[1] though it incidentally settled for the time the question of the definition of territorial waters, except as regards Norway and Sweden, who objected to the three-mile limit and therefore would be no party to the Convention.   After the war the definition of "territorial waters" and the distance limit will present more difficulties than ever, and not as regards fishery questions only.

Before 1860, therefore, there was no important fresh legislation except the Convention of 1839, nor was there as yet any very noticeable development of steam fishing.   On the other hand, no serious steps had as yet been taken to study the life-history of the fish; pollution of every description was rife on the coasts as in the rivers, and science had not yet been applied to the question of the preservation and increase of this great source of national food supply, though politics had had their say for centuries. But a change was, fortunately, at hand, and in 1860 a far-reaching step was taken by the appointment of a Royal Commission, consisting of Professor Huxley, Sir John Caird and Lord Eversley (then Mr. Shaw-Lefevre), to inquire into the condition of the British sea-fisheries, the desirability of the methods then in use for fishing, notably beam-trawling, and the value

[1] *Quarterly Review*, 1913, p. 450.

of the existing laws regulating the fisheries.
One of the most important witnesses was Frank
Buckland, to whose exertions then and in his
strenuous after-life the position of the industry
to-day is largely due. The report appeared
in 1866, and embodied four main conclusions :
(1) that the supply of fish upon the British
coasts is increasing and can be further increased
by legislation ; (2) that beam-trawling in the
open sea is not injurious to the industry ;
(3) that all existing Acts should be repealed,
and " unrestricted freedom of fishing be permitted hereafter " ; (4) that all fishing boats
" should be registered and licensed," and to
that end should bear letters and numbers by
which each should be distinguished.

Two years later, by the Sea Fisheries Act
of 1868, the recommendations of the Commission were carried into effect, and the registration
of fishing boats was regulated by an Order in
Council during the following year.

Buckland's appointment as Inspector of
Salmon Fisheries in 1876 had results far exceeding the limits of his official position. The
dream of his life had been the improvement of
British fisheries and fishermen, and in his visits
to seaports and rivers up and down the
country he was enabled to add to his exhibition
of objects connected with the fisheries at the
South Kensington Museum and to pave the
way for the International Fisheries Exhibition
of 1883. In 1878, moreover, he, with Messrs.

different times upon the different coasts instead of catching them at one season only and then turning their attention to line-fishing. Steam trawling has also increased in enormous proportions round the coasts of England. A steam drifter will take over a ton of herring with 500 square feet of nets as compared with under half a ton with the same spread of nets if used by a sailing vessel. In 1907, when Holland had only 81 steam trawlers, France had 224, Germany 239, and England and Wales no less than 1,317, the total number of steam trawlers in Germany and Holland in 1905 scarcely exceeding the mere additions to the British fleet in 1906 (" Encyclopædia Britannica," 11th ed., Vol. X., p. 430). In 1904, the value of the herring caught by British trawlers was £1,870,000, while that of Holland in the same year was £575,000 and that of Germany £220,000. Before the war there were, however, distinct indications that the North Sea and the Scottish North Sea ports were being less widely fished than before, since other and more profitable fishing grounds beyond the North Sea were available. When we read, with regard to the North Sea, of " a gross decrease of more than 25 per cent. in 1905 as compared with 1903, and, in relation to the catching power employed, to an average decrease of $2\frac{1}{2}$ cwts. per boat per diem " (*op. cit.*, p. 430), the matter was obviously serious, but any attempt to forecast the

future or to reinstate the North Sea as the
foremost fishing ground of Europe is at present
impossible, since the effect of the war on the
fisheries cannot be foreseen. Mines, submarines,
noise, disturbance, incessant patrolling of the
waters—all these make the question obscure
and doubtful, and it will be some years after
peace has been declared before the future policy
of the country with regard to her fisheries can
take shape. There is also the possibility that
the three-mile limit may disappear, to be
replaced by a ten or even a twenty-mile limit.

Certain reforms are obviously urgent, but
they will be clearer if we consider not only the
particulars already given but the statistics
of the year 1913 relating to the export trade
in herrings as it was, before the present war
had upset all calculations and all precedents.

In 1913, then, we actually exported from the
United Kingdom cured and salted herring to
the value of nearly £5,500,000 sterling, repre-
senting about 3,000,000,000 fish, of which Russia
and Germany together took nearly 80 per cent.,
while in the same year we landed in the United
Kingdom 3,500,000,000 fresh herring, worth
about £4,500,000 sterling. Germany and Russia
were our best export markets, these countries
taking pickled, but very few smoked herrings,
while Italy and Greece took them smoked and
salted, but not pickled; the British Colonies
and Dependencies took the fish in various forms,
including a large number tinned. Germany

already cited, entitled " The Territorial Waters
and the Sea Fisheries," for a summary of the
position as it was before the war, and for the
reforms which then seemed advisable. The
state of the fisheries, the legal position of
foreign poachers, the changes in the position
of fishing and trawling and in the use of
drifters, the strong position of the Scottish
and Irish Fisheries Boards as compared with
that of the English Board of Agriculture and
Fisheries—these are among the subjects dealt
with. The position of foreign poachers will
be settled by the war ; the limit of territorial
waters must be increased ; the condition of the
fisheries cannot be foreseen. But even in these
days of stress it is clear that reforms in the
administration of the fisheries must come, that
foreign vessels must no longer share or steal
the privileges of the English fishing fleets as of
right, that the scientific study of pisciculture
must be carried further, that improved means
of cold storage, curing and distribution must be
adopted for fish, and that the herring must
become more and more a staple article of food,
being more truly that which Kingsley said of
the salmon, " of all Heaven's gifts of food, the
one to be most carefully protected."

We have now traced, in outline at least, the
part played by the herring in the history of
Britain, and therefore in the building of the
Empire. The search for food led to the discovery

of his value in that respect, and this to his value as merchandise which was early perceived by the Hansards, who were glad to exchange other commodities for the invaluable herring ; out of the herring sprang the wealth and greatness of the Hansa League till Beuckel's discovery of a new method of curing raised the Dutch, through their fishing fleet, to the rank of the first mercantile nation of the world and gave Holland the first modern mercantile marine. This in its turn led to the struggle between Dutch and English in and after Cromwell's days, and by the passing of the Navigation Act of 1651 and the creation of our mercantile marine, to the rise of the British Navy and to the supersession of the Dutch as the leading naval power ; the British Navy and mercantile marine assisted the building up of our Colonial Empire, the possession of the carrying trade led to the expansion of our production of overseas raw materials and the development of overseas trade—this to the envy of Germany, who saw her opportunity in the repeal of the Navigation Acts in 1849 ; she began to build a mercantile marine and out of it a navy, and to plan a world empire to supersede our own by defeating us and gaining Dominion of the Sea, thereby realising the dream of List of dominating the trade of the world by control of colonial raw products. Hence one of the causes of the present war and its consequences.

Such is the House that Jack Herring built.

APPENDICES

The following methods of preparing herrings for the table are given by John Solas Dodd, 1752.

To Stew Herrings.

When your Herrings are scaled, washed, and the Fins cut off, put them in a Stewpan, with no Liquor but a quarter of a Pint of White Wine, some Mace, whole Pepper and Salt. When they are half stewed, put in some thick Cream, and a little piece of Butter dip'd in Flour; when that is melted, put in some Oisters with their Liquor; keep them often shaking till the Fish and Oisters are enough, or that the Oisters will break; squeese in a little Lemon, give them a Scald and pour them into a Dish.

To Pot Herrings.

Take any Number of Herrings, gut them and cut off their Heads, then put them in an Earthen Pot, lay them very close, and between every Layer of Herrings strew a little Salt; put in Cloves, Mace, whole Pepper and Nutmeg cut to Bits, not grated. Fill up the Pot with Vinegar and Water, and an Eighth part White Wine; cover it with brown Paper, tie it down and bake it with brown Bread. When cold 'tis fit to eat.

To pot herrings after they are pickled they must lay all Night in Milk, parboil them before putting into the Pot, adding more Vinegar.

To Bake Herrings.

Take thirty Herrings, scale them, cut off their Heads, put out their Roes, and wash them very clean, lay them to drain four or five Hours, and roll them in a dry Cloth, season them with Pepper and Salt, and lay them at their full Length in a long Venison Pot. When you have laid one Row, shred a large Onion very small and mix it with a little Cloves, Mace and Ginger cut small, and strew it all over the Herrings, and then another Row of Herrings and Seasoning, and so do till all is in the Pot; let it stand seasoned an Hour, then put in a Quart of Claret, and tie it over with Paper, and bake them.

To Make a Herring-Pye.

Take your Herrings split, headed, scalcd, boned and washed; then make a good Puff-paste, and lay your Dish or Pattipan, season your Herrings with spice, and lay a layer of Butter and a layer of Herrings, till all is in; then take three Anchovies, Eel, chop'd small, hard Yolks of Eggs, Marrow, sweet Herbs, a few Oisters, some small Pepper, grated Bread and Nutmeg. Make up the Forced-meat with raw Eggs, into Balls, some round; lay them about your Herrings; put butter over all, lid your pye, and an Hour will bake it.

Herrings the Spanish Way.

Take the Fish, take away their Heads, Tails, Fins and Guts, and soak them a Night in Vinegar, then wipe them dry, and score them on the Back very deep, then take Thyme chop'd very small, a little Mace and Nutmeg, mix them together and therewith fill the Scotches of the Fish; then tie them round with a Thread, and lay them on the Grid iron and baste them with Butter (or Oil if in Lent). Take care the fire is not too hot; turn them and baste till both Sides are brown; then when they are ready eat them with this Sauce, dissolve six Anchovies very well with half a Pound of Butter, three Spoonfuls of made Mustard, some Vinegar and a Clove of Garlick chop'd small.

To Pickle Herrings like Anchovies.

Take fresh Herrings, take out the Bone, and cut the Flesh into long Slices, of the Size of Anchovies, then to one Hundred of these Pieces take Pepper, Nutmeg and Petre Salt, each half an Ounce, half an Ounce of Mace, and half a Pound of Common Salt, beat all fine, and lay your fish in Layers, and between every Layer strew the seasoning, with Four or Five Bay leaves, then boil Red Wine, and pour in hot enough to cover them. Cover the Steam in with a Plate, and when cold tie them down close; and thus they exceed Anchovies.

To Make Herring-Soop.

Take eight large Herrings, skin and boil them in six Quarts of Water: When they are enough take them up, pick off the Flesh and put in the Bones. Take four more Herrings, a Piece of Lemon-Peel, a Bundle of Sweet Herbs, whole Pepper, two or three Blades of Mace, a little Horse Radish, the Crust of a Penny Loaf, and a little Parsley. Cover it close, and let it boil till there is about two Quarts, then strain it off, and add an Ounce of Vermicelly; set it on the Fire, and let it boil softly: In the meantime get a French Roll, cut a little Hole in the Top, take out the crumb, fry the Crust brown in Butter, take the Flesh of the Fish you laid by, cut it into little Pieces, put it into the Saucepan, with two or three Spoonsful of the

Soop, shake in a little Flour, put in a piece of Butter, a little Pepper and Salt, shake them together in the Saucepan till it is quite thick, then fill the Roll with it. Pour your Soop into your Dish; let the Roll swim in the Middle, and send it to the Table.

To Roast a Brace of Herrings.

Take two very large Herrings washed very clean, strew a little Salt hang them on the Spits of a Tin-Oven. Throw away all the water that comes from them for the first Half-hour; then throw on a little Nutmeg, Mace and Cloves, beat fine, and a little Salt; flour, and baste with Butter and Crumbs of Bread. When one side is done turn the other. Then have ready some Anchovy and Melted Butter, some of the Liver of the Fish boiled and bruised fine; mix it well with some Butter and two Yolks of Eggs, strain through a Sieve, and put them into the Saucepan again with a few Shrimps, or pickled Oisters, the juice of a Lemon and a little Red Wine. Pour it into the Pan that you put your Herrings in, and stir all together; then pour it again into the Saucepan, keep it stirring, let it boil, and then serve it up, garnished with pickled Barberries.

To Broil Herrings.

Scale them, gut them, cut off the Heads, wash them clean; dry them in a cloth, flour them and broil them, but with your Knife score them a little. Take the Heads and mash them, boil them in stale Ale, with a little whole Pepper and Onion; let it boil a quarter of an Hour, then strain it, thicken it with Butter and Flour, and a good deal of Mustard. Lay the Fish in the Dish, and pour the Sauce into a Bason.

To Fry Herrings.

Clean the Herring, fry them in Butter, have ready a good many Onions peeled and cut thin. Fry them of a light Brown, with the Herrings, lay your Herrings in the Dish, and the Onions round, and Butter and Mustard in a Cup.

To Dress Red Herrings and Cabbage.

Boil your cabbage tender, then put it into a Saucepan, and chop it with a Spoon; put in a good piece of Butter, keep it stirring lest it burn. Take some red Herrings and split them open, and Toast them before the Fire, till they are hot through; lay the Cabbage in a Dish, and the Herring on it, and send it to the Table hot.

To Make a Virginia Trout.

Take pickled Herrings, cut off their Heads, and lay the Bodies two Days and Nights in Water; then wash them well, season them with Mace, Cinnamon, Cloves, Pepper and a little red Sanders. Then lay them close in a pot with a little Onion chopt small and strewed between them, then put in a Pint of Claret, and cover them with a double Paper tied on the Pot, then bake them. They are to be eaten cold.

To Stew Herrings.

Take half a dozen large Herrings; gut them and put a Lump of Butter in the Belly of each of them, put them in your Fish Kettle, pour in half a Pint of boiling Vinegar, then put in a Pint and a half of Red Wine, and a Pint of Boiling Water. Season the whole with Salt, Pepper, sweet Herbs, Parsley and Shallot; and let it stew slowly, and when ready serve up.

A Ragout of Soft Roes.

Take some soft roes, and let them lay a little while in Warm Water. Then put in a Stew-pan some melted Butter, Mushrooms, Truffles slic'd, and sweet Herbs; fry it a little, season it with Salt and Pepper, moisten it with Gravy, and let it Stew over a slow Fire. When stewed take off the Fat, and then put in the Roes; let it stay till they are enough, and serve up hot.

A Terrine of Herrings.

Take your Herrings, gut them, cut off the Heads and Fins, and cut them in long slices, seasoned with Pepper, Salt, and a little fine Spice; place these Slices in a stew-pan, and let it stew over a slow Fire; being stewed, take off the Cover, Skim it well, and pour into it a Ragout of soft Roes. Let it be well relish'd, and serve it up hot in your Terrine.

A Pye of Soft Roes.

Take your Roes blanch'd, then lay a Puff-paste Crust at the botton of the Pan, and put over it a Stuffing of forc'd Meat; place your soft Roes over it with Mushrooms and Truffles, season them with Pepper, Salt and sweet Herbs. Lay over them some Butter with Slices of Bacon, cover your Pye with Crust, colour it with Eggs, and bake it. When baked, take it out and open it. Take out the Fat with the Slices of Bacon, pour in a Ragout, and serve up hot.

A Pudding with Pickled Herrings.

Take your pickled herrings, soak them in Water twenty-four Hours. Then take four Pounds of Crumb of a new Loaf, let it be soaked in Cream, and then boiled; then boil your Fish well, bone, skin, and mince them small, and put in your boiled Crumbs with a Dozen Eggs and Two Pound of Butter. Season it with a little Parsley, sweet Basil, Nutmeg, Shallot, and a glass of Sack. All these things being mixed together, tie them up in a Napkin, and put them in boiling Water, let it have a good colour, and serve up hot.

BOIL'D PICKLED HERRING WITH CARROTS.

Take your large Herrings, soak them well, boil some small Carrots in Water, and throw your Fish cut into slices into it. Your Fish being done, dish it up, and with each Fish two or three Carrots. Take some Parsley wash'd and cut small, which put in a Sauce-boat, and melted Butter in another, and serve up.

N.B. Some put Mustard in the Butter.

A FRICASSE OF ROES.

Take a quantity of soft Roes blanch'd, cut them into Dice; put a lump of Butter in a Stew-pan, and toss it up with an Onion cut small. After that put in your Dice, and give them two or three Tosses; this done, put a little Flour over them, moisten them with a little Fish Broth, seasoned with Salt, Pepper, sweet Herbs, and fine Spice; and let them stew gently. Being done, thicken it with Yolks of Eggs, Parsley cut small, and a Dash of Vinegar, serv'd up hot.

Note. That pickled Roes will do as well steep'd in Water to unsalt them, and omitting Salt in the seasoning.

J. S. Dodd states that " The Herring is likewise endued with Medicinal Qualities . . . for application to the Soles of the Feet." Dodd gives many ways in which remedies made from herrings can be used internally and externally.

The word Lowestoft appears in Dodd's book as " Loestoff." In the map provided by Ives in his " Garianonum " it appears as " Leaystofe. " Its modern local pronunciation is as if it were spelt " Low-stoff." Fifty years or so ago it was pronounced " Lestoff." In Domesday Book it is entered under the name " Loth-Wistoft," a Saxon or Scandinavian name, *i.e.*, the green-knoll (Toft) by the slow flowing stream (Loth).

A GLUT.—Sixty million herrings were landed at Yarmouth in *one single day*, 22 Oct., 1907. One hundred million had been caught but, as there was not enough quay space, incoming boats left Yarmouth and went to Grimsby to unload. One boat brought in a quarter of a million herrings. The price landed on the quay opened at 12*s*. and fell to 3*s*. per 1,000 herrings. At 12*s*. per 1,000 three pounds weight of herrings cost one penny.

In 14 weeks, from mid-Sept. to 20 Dec., 1913, there were landed at Yarmouth 825 million herrings, weighing 157,000 tons, valued at one million sterling landed. The prices ranged from 7*s*. to 91*s*. per 1,000. Most of the herrings went to Russia and Germany. Large quantities of smoked herrings were sold to Italy, Greece, Turkey, the Levant and Palestine. The like of the Yarmouth fishing in 1913 had never been known in any other port in the world.

In 1915 120 million herrings were landed at Yarmouth. The average value was 80*s*. per 1,000; the prices varied from 40*s*. to 146*s*. France and America bought largely.

In 1917 only 5,700 tons of herrings were landed in England ; average value about 87*s*. per 1,000, about 2½*d*. per lb.

STATUTES

THE following are some of the principal Acts of Parliament relating to fisheries and fishing from Edward I. to George I.

13 Edw. I., c. 47. Salmon, etc., in defence.

31 Edw. III., Stat. 2, c. 1. Herrings sold at sea.

31 Edw. III., Stat. 2. Herrings, Yarmouth, etc.

31 Edw. III., Stat. 2. Stockfish of St. Botolph, salmon of Berwick, fish and wines of Bristuit, etc.

31 Edw. III., Stat. 3, c. 1. Fishery, Blackeney, and the coasts of Satterly, Winton, etc., in the county of ——

31 Edw. III., Stat. 3, c. 2. Fair at Blakeney, lob, ling, cod, orgies, selling, etc., their nets, etc., Norfolk.

35 Edw. III. Buying and selling herrings, Yarmouth.

4 Rich. II. Fishmongers' trade laid open.

6 Rich. II., c. 10. Fish and victuals to be sold by aliens in London, enforced by Hen. I., c. 17; 14 Hen. IV., c. 4.

7 Rich. II., c. 11. Fishers, vintners, and victuallers coming to London to be in the rule of the Lord Mayor and aldermen. 31 Edw. III., Stat. 1, c. 1. (N.B.) repeals the Statutes of 5 Rich. II., c. 4, and 6 Rich. II., c. 11 and 12, touching victuallers in London.

31 Rich. II., c. 19, confirms Stat. 13 Edw. I., c. 47, and appoints conservators of it, etc.

17 Rich. II., c. 9. All justices of peace to be conservators of 13 Edw. I., c. 47, and 13 Rich. II., c. 9. These conservators to appoint subconservators, etc.

2 Hen. IV., c. 15. Penalty on fastening trinck and other nets over the Thames and other rivers; trinckers may fish lawfully.

14 Hen. IV., c. 4. Penalty on disturbing aliens selling their fish.

22 Edw. IV., c. 2. Salmon vessels, salmon packed, grill packed, herrings packed, sold in barrels, etc., eels barrelled, etc. Length, etc., of barrelled fish, thokes, etc. Tale fish, their length, etc.

11 Hen. VII., c. 23. What gaugers, packers, and searchers of barrelled salmon, herrings, eels, etc., are entitled to, with penalty on their offending, etc.

31 Hen. VIII., c. 2, s. 2. Penalty on fishing in ponds, etc., against the will of the owners. See Eliz., c. 21 ; 2 & 3 Edw. VI., c. 6, s. 3. Penalty on admirals taking money, doles, etc., of fishermen or merchants, for licences to pass to voyages for fish, etc.

5 Eliz., c. 1. Penalty on fishing in ponds, etc., against the owner's consent.

5 Eliz., c. 5. No toll for sea-fish except on Kingston-upon-Hull ; penalty on herring or sea-fish, not well salted and packed, and cod, and ling, to be imported loose, and not in barrels.

5 Eliz., c. 17. A general provision for preserving of the spawn, brood, and fry of fish, made perpetual by Car. II., c. 4.

39 Eliz., c. 10. Exporting of herrings bought in this realm. Customs to be paid by aliens for selled fish and herrings. Penalty on importing or salting bad salt fish, or herrings. See 43 Eliz., c. 9.

1 Jac. I., c. 23, s. 3, relates to the taking of herring, pilchard and other sea fish in the counties of Somerset, Devon, and Cornwall.

3 Jac. I., c. 11. No weirs along the sea-coast, and penalty on killing, etc., of the brood, etc., of sea-fish, assize, etc., of sea-nets.

13 & 14 Car. II., c. 2, s. 36, relates to the exportation of fish into any ports of the Mediterranean.

BIBLIOGRAPHY

AMERICAN Philosophical Society in Philadelphia, Transactions of the. 1771, etc.

An Act for settling of Differences between the Townes of Great and Little Yarmouth, touching the lading and unlading of Herrings and other Merchandizes and Commodityes. 1676, 1677.

An exact and authentic Account of the White Herring Fishery in Zetland by the Dutch. 1750.

ANDERSON, JAMES. "An Account of the Present State of the Hebrides and Western Coasts of Scotland, with hints for encouraging the Fisheries, being the substance of a report to the Lord of the Treasury." Edinburgh, 1785.

BARKER, SAMUEL. "The Examination of . . . at a Meeting of the Directors of the British Society for extending the Fisheries, etc."
"Reports on the State. of the British Herring Fisheries, 1798—1800," No. 2. 1798, pp. 254—5.

BEAUJON, A. "The History of the Dutch Sea Fisheries" (Fisheries Exhibition Literature, Vol. IX., Prize Essays, Part II.). 1884.

BERTRAM, J. G. "The Harvest of the Sea." 3rd ed. Murray. 1873.

BEUDEKER, C. "Germania Inferiora . . . Kaertboeck van de XVII. Nederlandtsche Provincien," Vol. VII. 1718.

BLOUNT. "History of Strange Tenures of Lands."

BOWLES, THOS. GIBSON. "Sea Law and Sea Power." 1910.

"British Channel Fisheries Report." (Blue Book.) 1833.

BUCKLAND, FRANK. "The Fisheries of Norfolk." 1875.

BUCKLAND, WALPOLE and YOUNG. "Report presented to Parliament on the Herring Fisheries of Scotland." 1878.

BURROUGHS, SIR JOHN. "The Soveraignty of the British Seas. Proved by Records, History and Municipall Lawes of this Kingdome. Written in the year 1633. 1651. Repr. in Gerard Malynes' 'Consuetudo Lex Mercatoria; or the Antient Law-Merchant.'" Ed. 1686, and again in 1729.

CAWOOD, F. "Essay or Scheme towards the Establishing and Improving the Fishery of Great Britain."

CHAFFERS, W. "Marks and Monograms on, etc., etc., Pottery, etc." 8th ed. 1897.

COLLINS, J. "Salt and Fishery." 1682.

Commons, House of : Two Reports from the Select Committee of the House of Commons, appointed in 1785 to enquire into the State of the British Fisheries. 1786.

Seven Reports from the same Committee on the State of the British Fisheries, and on the most Effectual means for their Improvement, Encouragement and Extension. 1786.

Another Report. 1798.

COUCH, JONATHAN, F.L.S. "A History of Fishes of the British Isles." 1877.

CUNNINGHAM, W., D.D. "The Growth of English Industry and Commerce during the Early and Middle Ages." Cambridge University Press. 1896.

DAY, FRANCIS, F.L.S. "Fishes of Great Britain and Ireland." 1880—4. 2 Vols.

"The Commercial Sea Fishes of Great Britain." London. 1883. (Not in British Museum.)

DE CAUX, J. W. "The Herring and the Herring Fishery." 1881.

DEE, DR. JOHN. "The Petty Navy Royal." 1577.

DE JONG, D., H. KOBEL EN M. SALIETH. "Nieuwe Beschryving der Walvisfangst en Haringvisschery." Amsterdam. 1792.

DE JONGH (D.) and SALLIETH (M.). "Atlas de Zeehavens der Bataafsche Republiek . . . Mitsgaders de Asbeeldingen van de Haringvisscherÿ." Amsterdam, 1805.

DODD, JAMES SOLAS. "Essay towards a Natural History of the Herring." 1752.

DONOVAN, EDWARD. "The Natural History of British Fishes." 5 Vols. 1802—8.

DUFF, R. W., M.P. "Herring Fisheries of Scotland, 1883." (In "Papers of the International Fisheries Exhibition of 1883.")

DU HAMEL DU MONCEAU (M.), Inspecteur Général de la Marine. "Traité Général des Pesches, et Histoire des Poissons qu'elles fournissent, tant pour la subsistence des Hommes, que pour plusieurs autres Usages qui ont rapport aux Arts et au Commerce." Paris. 1769, 1772 and 1777. "Le Hareng," Vol. II., sect. iii., pl. I.—XVI.

DUNDONALD, ARCHIBALD, NINTH EARL OF. "Thoughts on the Manufacture and Trade of Salt, the Herring Fisheries, etc." 1784.
    "The Present State of the Manufacture of Salt, Explained." 1786, 2 edd.

ELDER, J. R. "The Royal Fishery Companies of the Seventeenth Century." Maclehose, Glasgow. 1912. (1911.)

"Encyclopædia Britannica." 11th ed., art. "Fisheries."

FEA, J. "Considerations on the Fisheries in the Scotch Islands." 1775. Reprinted, Edinburgh, 1884.

"Fish Trades Gazette, The."

"Fisheries Revived, The. Britain's Hidden Treasure Discovered." 1750.

FORBES, DUNCAN, OF CULLODEN. "Some Considerations on the Present State of Scotland." 1744.

FRASER, ROBERT. "A Review of the Domestic Fisheries of Great Britain and Ireland." 1818.

GENTLEMAN, TOBIAS. "The Way to Wealth and to employ ships' mariners, or a plaine description what great profite it will bring into the Commonwealth

BIBLIOGRAPHY 191

of England, by the erecting, building and adventuring of busses to sea a-fishing. With a true Relation of the inestimable wealth that is yearely taken out of his Maiestie's seas by the Hollanders by their numbers of Busses, Pinkes and Live boates . . . Fisherman and Mariner." 1614. New Edition, London, 1660 ; reprinted in " An Harleian Miscellany," 1744, 1808 ; abridged by Gerrard Malynes. 1622.

HÉRUBEL. " Sea Fisheries." 1908—12.

HITCHCOCK, ROBERT. " A Politique Platt for the Honour of the Prince, the Great Profite of the Publique State, reliefe of the Poor, preservation of the Rule, reformation of Roges and Idle Persons, and the wealthe of thousands that knowes not howe to live, by Robert Hitchcock, Gentleman." 1580.

HOLDSWORTH, E. W. H. " Sea Fisheries." 1877.

HUXLEY, T. H. " The Herring, a Lecture delivered at the National Fishery Exhibition at Norwich, April 21st, 1881." (" Scientific Memoirs of T. H. Huxley," Vol. IV., ch. 27. 1902.)

" International Fisheries Exhibition, Papers of the, London." 1883.

IVES, JOHN. " Remarks upon the Garianonum of the Romans." 1774.

KNOX, JOHN, Bookseller. " A View of the British Empire, more especially Scotland, etc." 1784, 2 edd. 3rd ed. enlarged, 1785. 2 Vols.

KNOX, JOHN. " Observations on the Northern Fisheries." 1786.

LANGSDORFF. " Herring Roe in Norfolk Sound." *Harper's Magazine*, Vol. II., p. 108.

L'ESTRANGE, SIR ROGER. " A Discourse of the Fishery, Briefly laying open not only the Advantages, and Facility of the Undertaking, but likewise the Absolute Necessity of it, in Order to the Well-being both of King and People." 1674. The following is the bibliography of L'Estrange's Discourse :—

WILSON, JAMES, F.R.S.E. "A Voyage round the Coasts of Scotland and the Isles." 2 vols. 1842. Revised, 2 vols. 1853.

WOOD, SIR H. T. "History of the Royal Society of Arts." 1913.

ZIMMERN, HELEN. "The Hansa Towns." 1889.

INDEX

ABBEY, Saint Edmondsbury, 59
" Aberdeen fish," 74
Aberdeen haul of herrings, 22
Association of Chambers of Commerce, 23, 24, 114
Association to Capture Herring, 1654...115

" BACONED " herrings, 92
Banff Journal, 42
Battle of Herrings, 89
Beaujon, A., " History of the Dutch Sea Fisheries," 102
Beaumont and Fletcher, quoted, 36
Beccles, 59
Beuckels, 101
Bible, quoted by Scottish fishermen, 44
Bibliography of seventeenth century writings on fisheries, 122
Bloater, 34 ; derivation, 35 ; how to prepare, 35
Board of Trade, 24
Boswell, " Tour," 134
Bread in 1800...161
Brighton fishermen, superstition, 44
" Britain's Buss," by E. S., 1615...97
British White Herring Fishery Company, 132
Browne, Sir T., at the Bury St. Edmunds Assizes, 46
Buckland, F., 167, 168
Burroughs, Sir J., " Soveraignty of the British Seas," 121
Busses, 96

" CADGER," 55
Cambridge, 85
Canning, E., the murderess, 129
Carlyle, on grilled herrings, 41
Chaffers, W., " Marks and Monograms," 143
Chanty, fishing, 21
Charles I., patent granted by, 99 ; has *The Sovereign* built, 109
Charles II., 116
Clausson, P., on the fisheries at Bohuslän, 44
Clupea, C. alba, whitebait, 27 ; *C. harengus*, the herring, 22 ;
    C. pilchardus, the pilchard, 27 ; *C. spratus*, the sprat, 27
Cod, great eaters of herring, 30, 31
Cold storage, 48
" Coshganger " or " cosher," 55
" Cow, Coloured, The," 82
" Cran," a measure, 76
Cromwell, his Navigation Laws, 57, 68
Croyland, Charter of, 76

" Kings and Queens," red-finned herrings, 45
Kingsley, C., on the salmon, 174
Kipper, 40 ; derivation, 40 ; how served, 41

LACÉPÈDE, quoted, 68
Last-burden, herring measure, 75
Lawes, Sir J., on fish as food, 22
Lent, licence to eat flesh, 98
L'Estrange, R., " A Discourse of the Fishery," 120
Lockman, the " Herring Poet," 133
Lübeck, chief town of Hanseatic League, 67 ; best money in
    the Middle Ages, 69 ; quartered herrings in arms, 70

Mare Clausum, by Selden, 106
Mare Liberum, by Grotius, 108
Marvell, A., quoted, 69, 115, 124
" Matties," from the Dutch, 55
Meat, increase in consumption of, 51
" Militia-men," Yarmouth red herrings, 36

NAOGEORGUS, " Popish Kingdome," quoted, 90
Nashe, T., his " Lenten Stuffe," quoted, 37
Navigation Act, 1651...113
Navy, British, 113
Nets, beam trawl, 31 ; drift, 32
Norfolk Sound, methods of securing herring roe, 41
Norwegian fishing in early times, 59
Norwich, 60, 62, 65, 73, 90
Notes and Queries, 42

OEHLANDSCHLAEGER, " Gods of the North," quoted, 90

PEACOCK, " Crotchet Castle," quoted, 137 ; " Misfortunes of
    Elphin," 101, *note*
Pepys, Diary, quoted, 119
Pickled herrings in Stornoway, 47. *See also under* " Herring."
Polluted water, shunned by herrings, 28
Pound sterling, 69
Prices in 1763...138
Puckle, J., " England's Interests," 124

Quarterly Review, " Territorial Waters and Sea Fisheries," 174

RALEIGH, Sir W., " Observations concerning Trade with the
    Dutch and other Foreign Nations," 94
Report by Buckland and others, on Scottish Herring Fisheries,
    168
Royal Fishery Company, 116
Russell, J., " Boke of Nurture," 1450...41

SABBATH, observance among fishermen, 42, 43
Salt, for curing herrings, 47, 103 ; analysed, 146 ; restrictions
    on, 151

Salted herrings, cooking of, 53 ; a form of currency, 70 ; method of, Beuckel's, 101

Scottish fisheries and fishing rights, 85, 125—127, 135 ; Loch Hourn, 139 ; Moray Firth closed against trawling, 169 ; cured herring trade, 163

" Seas, Freedom of the," 106

Selden, *Mare Clausum*, 108

" Ship-money," 57, 110—112

Society of Arts, 162, 163

Solinus, on the Hebrides, 58

Spectator, Addison's, 55, 56

Spriggs, E. L., Table of fish calories and prices, 52

Statistics of fish, 1909—1913...49 ; of herrings, 25, 26

Sunday fishing, 42

Superstitions, 42—47

" Sussex Highways and Byways," quoted, 44

TABLE of fish calories and prices, 52

Territorial waters, question of limit, 171, 174

VENTJAGERS, Dutch fishing yachts, 104

Victual Brothers, 82

WAR-TIME prices for herrings, 173

Weights and measures, herring, 75, 76

West Indies, export of herrings to, 142

" White " herring, 41

Witchcraft, hanging for, 46, 47

YARMOUTH, arms of the town, 37 ; Yarmouth bloater, 34 ; Yarmouth herrings, 34 ; best in autumn and late spring, 34 ; beginning of the fisheries, 58 ; affected by Tartar inroads in Europe, 70

Yarmouth Charter, 1286...73

Yarmouth dialect, " Yarmouth capons," 37 ; " Go foreign," 47

Yarmouth Herring Fair, 71, 164

THE WHITEFRIARS PRESS, LTD.,
LONDON AND TONBRIDGE.